SMOKE

SMOKE

A WOLF'S STORY

◆

Melanie Jane Banner

◆

Illustrations by

Kveta

Moulin

To my parents, Rupert and Shelagh Trim;
and the loyal friends who have stood by me,
during ten years of ME.

◆

Moulin Publishing Limited
P. O. Box #560
Norval, Ontario
Canada L0P 1K0

Canadian Cataloguing in Publication Data

Banner, Melanie Jane, 1952–
Smoke: a wolf's story

ISBN 1-896867-08-1

1. Wolves – Juvenile fiction   I. Kveta   II. Title.

PZ7. B22m 1997   j823'.914 C96-900730–5

Printed and bound in Canada
1 2 3 4 5   ML   00 99 98 97

Cover and text design by Counterpunch/Linda Gustafson
Cover and text illustrations by Kveta

PREFACE

If you're very lucky, every once in while, you meet some-one who becomes a truly special friend. When young Zan meets Smoke, he soon discovers he has found such a friend. Melanie Banner's wonderful story takes you along on Zan and Smoke's exciting journey together from Smoke's puppyhood, secretly stashed away in Zan's bedroom, to their perilous life on the streets. Through danger, excitement, and fun, Zan and Smoke constantly look out for one another. Then, as their adventure reaches its climax, Zan is faced with a difficult decision. Smoke has become Zan's best friend. He has also grown into a healthy young wolf, a wild animal who needs space and the companionship of his own kind. What will Zan do?

For generations, the wolf has been cast as the villain in many stories – a fictional creature which has very little in common with the real animal. Here, Smoke and Zan get the opportunity to help set the record straight. Through Smoke, we see the playful and intelligent side of wolves, as well as their determination to protect those who are close to them. By the end of the story, you will be rooting for Smoke, and for wolves everywhere.

Alison Hood
Born Free Foundation

PART ONE

THE PUPPY

CHAPTER ONE

"I'm sorry, Zan, but *no*," Mrs. Makepeace said firmly, for the umpteenth time. "You know this house is far too small; we're all out most of the day, and your father needs his sleep. Anyway, we can't possibly afford to feed a dog – it would eat us out of house and home. Why not have a nice little hamster instead?"

"Can't afford it, can't afford it!" Zan shouted back childishly. "So when *can* we afford it?" He knew he was being unreasonable, for both his parents worked very hard. But sometimes he longed for a puppy of his own so much, it physically *hurt!* And anyway, whoever heard of a *hamster* being man's best friend?

He flung his knife and fork down on the plate with a clatter and, leaving his supper half-eaten, he scraped back his chair and rushed out of the room.

"Alexander!" his father cried angrily, but Mrs. Makepeace reached out to touch his arm.

"Let him go," she told her husband gently.

Kibby, Zan's younger sister, heaved a sigh. She had watched this scene a hundred times before. Mealtimes were no fun at all when everyone was cross.

◆

Zan ran into his bedroom and slammed the door behind him. He hurled himself onto his bed and gazed around the room. Newly decorated and still smelling of paint, it was an unusual bedroom, for it had once been the main sitting room, and the largest room in the house. Now it was his own private den, while everyone else slept upstairs.

Zan had been allowed to stick posters on his walls. Lots of wildlife, and his favourite football stars. A brightly coloured blind covered the window, displaying a patch of lush tropical rainforest. The blind matched his duvet. In fact, he preferred to look at the rainforest rather than the view outside. For outside, there was really no view to speak of.

His bedroom window looked out onto a narrow alley-way, edged by red brick walls. Once, Zan's Uncle Kevin had jokingly called it Tin Can Alley because of all the litter there, and the name had stuck.

The alley walls had the usual smattering of unwanted graffiti. No sooner were they scrubbed clean than the graffiti returned, yet Zan never saw anyone drawing it. He often wondered if he might be allowed to paint the whole rainforest scene from his blind onto the ugly wall opposite, for he was an accomplished artist. But it would be a huge project. Maybe next year, when he had grown a little taller. . . .

Zan's eyes came to rest on his pride and joy: a brand new top-of-the-range computer! It was by far the most expensive item in the room – in the whole house, really – and it drew one's attention like a magnet. His parents could never have afforded to buy it for him, but earlier in the year, Zan had won it.

The children's favourite television programme, *Red Ensign*, had run a competition: "Draw your home town in fifty years' time." Zan nurtured a vivid imagination, and his fantasy painting of London had won first prize.

Toby Powers, the local butcher's son, was always begging Zan to let him use the computer. And, for the first time, Zan had revelled in possessing something which was the envy of others.

The Makepeaces were not exactly poor, but Zan's father, who was a night security guard, worked long and exhausting hours to provide for his wife and two children. Now that Zan was twelve and Kibby was eight, Mrs. Makepeace had found a job in a florist's shop to earn some extra money for the little luxuries they had all managed without for so many years.

"Well," Mr. Makepeace had joked when his wife brought home flamboyant bunches of unsold flowers, "we may not live like royalty, but we'll always have more fresh roses in the house than the Queen herself!"

Zan and Kibby had plenty to eat and warm clothes to wear, but it was difficult to keep up with all the expensive trends. If you didn't wear the right kind of shoes to school, you were teased like mad. Zan knew, because he didn't, and he was.

◆

It was nearly Christmas. For several months the city had been gathering momentum – the shops filling with garish decorations, their window displays offering every present imaginable. For the Makepeace family, it would be the most comfortable Christmas they had enjoyed in years. Business was blooming at the florist's, and after working extra hours Mrs. Makepeace had, for once, felt free to window-shop, spellbound by the myriad of gifts for sale everywhere. This year, they would all have presents to open on Christmas Day.

But Zan didn't want a present to open. Every birthday, and every Christmas, for as long as he could remember, he had wanted a puppy to share his life.

At the end of Tin Can Alley, there was a large area of waste ground where the neighbourhood children gathered to play. There, Zan often came across the local stray dogs – dogs of every shape, size, and colour, and he knew them all. They formed a motley pack, with the bigger, stronger mongrels in the upper ranks and a rag-tag collection of smaller creatures following along behind.

Zan had named the alley pack leader Thor, after the

God of Thunder. He was a huge, powerful black Labrador cross-breed, with a thick shaggy coat and a vicious warning snarl. He took his job as pack leader very seriously. Thor was nobody's fool, and nobody fooled with Thor!

Beneath him, several of the younger mongrels were much more friendly, and often allowed Zan to pet them. The boy always took them any scraps he could sneak out of the kitchen. His father frequently told him off for wasting good food.

Kibby and her best friend Lulu teased him whenever they saw him with the strays. "You'll catch fleas for sure. Oh, Zan, don't let them lick you – you'll get worms too! Mum will go bananas!" But Zan didn't care. He had never made friends easily. And he loved the dogs so much that, given half a chance, he would have smuggled the whole pack home to the warmth of his bedroom on cold winter nights. There was nothing else on earth quite like a happy yelp of welcome, a wagging tail, and the rasp of a warm tongue against your cheek to make you feel as if you'd won the lottery!

Zan had built up a special relationship with one dog in particular. She was a gentle long-haired black and white collie with only one ear. Goodness knows what had happened to the other. Zan had named her Jenna, and when she was around, Jenna was *his* dog. Of course, she ran with the pack seeking food, for Zan could not provide all she needed. But often, when he drew his blind in the morning, she would be sitting waiting for him in the alley, shaggy tail thumping the ground with pleasure as soon as she saw him. And it gave him a warm feeling to be loved, even if it was only the cupboard love of a neighbourhood stray.

Although a little thin, most of the dogs were in fine fettle. Thor was a wise leader, and he guided them well. There were plenty of small restaurants and cafés in the suburb of Sunfield where the pack found, or stole, enough food to survive. Some kindly café owners even gave them their scraps, for the odds and ends would only have gone for pig-swill anyway. Thus, the dinner menu was always varied. Sometimes stale buttered burger buns, sometimes spaghetti, sometimes even soggy but exotic leftovers from the Mah Jong Chinese Restaurant down the road. In particular, Jenna savoured the crispy pancakes with sweet and sour sauce. But Mr. Wong always clapped his hands if he caught the dogs raiding his dustbins.

Zan thought the alley pack was quite fortunate. When he helped out at the local Dogs' Home, as he often did, he could hardly bear to watch all the poor creatures barking and howling as they jumped up and down in their cramped cages. But at least they were warm. The Tin Can Alley pack was footloose and fancy free, but winter was never an easy time for them.

◆

Kibby lay sprawled on the fake fur rug in front of the fire. Her father had left for work, and her mother was curled up on the sofa, reading the latest slushy romance from the library. Kibby shuffled her toes away from the hearth, because they were growing far too hot. "Toasted cheese!" Zan would have quipped, but he was not there. Ever since supper had ended in another argument and more bad feelings, Zan had been sulking in his room. Kibby could hear his computer.

The dispute had been about the same old subject – a puppy. As she sat watching the flames flickering red and yellow in the grate, Kibby decided to make one last attempt at sorting things out. Makepeace was her name, and making peace for the whole family was something she dearly wanted to do. Lulu would have teased her to bits, but it was worth a try.

At the top of a new piece of notepaper, she began to write in her neatest handwriting, her brow furrowed with concentration.

Dear Father Christmas,

Please, PLEASE could you send my brother, Alexander, a puppy for Christmas. And could Mum let him keep it. Just a teensy one will do, so it wouldn't eat much or get in Dad's way. And please, could it not smell or have fleas like the alley pack dogs. I'd HATE that. I hope you're not too busy to help, Father Christmas, because it's horrible when everyone fights. Thank you very much.

Love from

KATHLYN-ANN MAKEPEACE

XXX

P.S. I'd love a pony too please, but only a toy one with a bridle and saddle. There's no room here for a real one. They make such a mess, don't they?

Then she crumpled up the letter and threw it onto the fire, watching the smoke signals flowing quickly up the chimney where they disappeared into the darkness.

"There," she said, satisfied. "Finished!"

"What's that, dear?" her mother asked, not bothering to look up from her novel.

"Nothing," Kibby replied smugly. She stretched out sleepily across the rug and added more quietly, "That *must* have done it!"

Her grandmother had always told her: "If you believe hard enough, Kibby my dear, you can make *anything* happen." So for a moment or two, she sat in silence, believing as hard as she possibly could.

CHAPTER TWO

Christmas Day was the happiest of days – the best either Zan or Kibby could remember. Uncle Kevin and Aunt Josie came to stay, bringing Grandma Makepeace too. It was quite a squash to fit them all in, and both the children had to sleep on the floor. But that was half the fun, and anyway Kibby was far too excited to sleep.

The sitting-room was warm, noisy, and colourful, with a large artificial Christmas tree standing in one corner, courtesy of the florist's shop. Kibby had been allowed to decorate most of it herself, apart from the lights. This year, as a surprise, Mr. Makepeace had brought home a new set, in brilliant colours, which made the tree look very exotic. Zan had been rather disappointed they didn't keep exploding like the old ones. That had been much more entertaining, especially when it made his mother scream!

Before lunch, everyone opened presents. In no time at

all, the sitting-room was knee-deep in ribbons and wrapping paper.

To Kibby's delight, her largest parcel contained the model pony for which she had been longing – a glorious life-like dappled grey with a flowing silver mane and tail.

"Oh, thank you, Father Christmas!" she whispered softly to herself, then she trilled out loud, "Thanks, Mum and Dad! As it's freezing outside, I think I'll call him Frosty!" And, because it was Christmas Day, Zan decided not to tease her about it.

Of course the boy knew that there would be no puppy. But right up until the very last second, both he and Kibby had nursed just the smallest of hopes. However, Zan was not the least bit disappointed with his present. This year, as a treat, his parents had been able to afford a pair of the very latest in-line skates.

"Wow!" Zan cried, his eyes sparkling with pleasure as he opened the box. "*Thank* you! They're terrific, the best present I've ever had!"

There was far too much to eat, and after everyone had eaten far too much there was also plenty of food left over. When no one was looking, Zan carefully collected it up, cramming it into a bag for the alley pack: two cold roast potatoes, a piece of Christmas pudding, minus the old-fashioned sixpence (which Grandma had found and wished upon), a mince pie, and several other delicacies. When Mr. Makepeace tipped the leftover turkey skin into the dustbin, Zan slipped straight out of his bedroom window to rescue that too, and secretly tucked the carrier bag full of food into the flower box below the windowsill. There would be quite a feast for Jenna and her friends to enjoy.

The whole family trooped out into the alley after tea to watch Zan try out his new in-line skates. They cheered and clapped when, finally finding his balance, he began to race up and down in front of them. He swooped and glided, gradually gaining speed as his confidence built. Mrs. Makepeace glanced at her husband and smiled. The skates were an enormous success, and it was wonderful to see Zan so happy again.

By Boxing Day, Zan was something of an expert. Uncle Kevin and Aunt Josie had left for home with Grandma, and at last Mr. and Mrs. Makepeace had grown tired of watching their son as he twisted and turned, skating at breakneck speeds along the alley.

Finally, only Kibby remained, following him cautiously down the slippery pathway to the waste ground at the far end. She was wrapped up warmly in a new blue coat, with a woolly rainbow-hued scarf, her little button nose and her cheeks flushed pink in the cold. She still clutched Frosty tightly.

It was one of those rare and peculiar times when the entire city lay completely silent, as though no one but the two children lived there at all. The sky was quite clear, the last of a tangerine sunset just fading in the west, giving way to the timeless blue-black of the night.

"Come on, Zan, it's freezing. It'll be dark soon," Kibby called. "We'll be in dead trouble!"

"Go home, then," Zan told her. "Jenna's sure to come soon. I'll be along in a little while." He gathered speed and turned sharply to the left. He did not see the large pineapple can which lay directly in his path until it was too late.

Zan's blades caught on the edge of the can, and he spun in a complete somersault and landed with a thud beside a new heap of rubbish.

Kibby scuttled over to him. "What an amazing crash!" she cried. "You went right over! Have you broken anything? Can you see any bones?"

But Zan was already sitting up and rubbing his ankles. Luckily his pads and helmet had protected him from serious injury.

"Don't be dumb. I've just twisted my foot." He grinned sheepishly. "Should've looked where I was going. Don't worry, kid. I'll be fine."

Kibby seemed a little disappointed. "Oh. Well, I'm going home then. What a clumsy old clogs you are. And *don't* call me 'kid'!"

"Sorry, kiddie!"

"And I'm not 'kiddie' either. I'm *Kibby!*"

"What's that, kiddie? Can't hear a word you're saying."

"I'll call you *Alec*. I will! Mr. Smart Alec!"

"Don't you dare, or I'll make you another of those apple pie beds. Boy, did you squeal, when you found all the snails!"

"Mum said if you ever made up my bed like that again, there'd be no TV for weeks. And she *meant* it!"

"You're such a little tell-tale. Brrr, it's freezing. Go home, kiddio, before your nose turns blue and drops off!"

"I hope your ears do too!"

Christmas was well and truly over now, and Zan and Kibby were back to their usual banter. Although, for a brother and little sister, they got along remarkably well most of the time, and they had always looked out for each other in their parents' absence. But Zan would never have admitted it to the boys at school, or they'd tease him to death.

Just as Kibby turned to go, she heard the faintest of whimpers.

"Was that you, Zan? Are you hurt after all?"

"'Course not – don't be daft!"

"Well, I heard *something*."

"You're hearing things!" Zan taunted. "You're loopy!"

At that moment, they both heard Jenna's excited bark. The collie came bounding across the frozen ground to greet them. Her tail began to wag madly as soon as she smelled the leftover turkey Zan had hidden for her.

"Happy Christmas. Good girl." They both hugged her and patted her soft back. Zan got up and retrieved the bag of turkey skin and placed it on the ground for her. Jenna began wolfing down the food. She knew that the faster she ate, the less chance there was of anyone else stealing her supper.

"You'll be sick," Kibby warned smugly, watching intently to see if she would be.

But Jenna wasn't sick. When she had finished almost every scrap, her attention was drawn to the pile of rubbish where Zan had fallen. She padded around it, sniffing carefully, and then gave a single worried bark.

"What is it, old girl?" Zan asked, stroking her head gently.

By this time, one or two of the other dogs from the alley pack were gathering round too, licking up the crumbs from Jenna's feast, and nudging Zan in case he had any more food. He petted them all in turn. Jenna was nuzzling a black plastic bag now, whining anxiously and pawing it gently.

"Come on then, nosey!" Zan teased her. "Let's have a look."

He pulled the sacking open and gasped.

"What is it?" Kibby asked urgently.

"Stand back! Don't look!" Zan ordered. "It's four newborn pups. I think they may all be frozen, poor things."

"Not all of them," Kibby said, pushing fearlessly past two of the larger mongrels. "I heard a noise, if you remember, and so did Jenna. I wasn't imagining it at all."

"Shut up and let me think."

Kibby crouched down beside her brother as he peered into the sack. Jenna pushed her face in between them, keen to have a look as well. Puzzled, the other dogs made a wider circle around them. As the little group stood and stared in silent amazement at the tiny orphans on that

bitter December evening, they made a touching picture.

"So Father Christmas must have seen my letter after all," Kibby breathed quietly, wanting to believe it and prove Lulu wrong.

"Pardon?"

"Oh, nothing. What are we going to do?"

"The pups are in a terrible state," Zan said sadly. "I can't believe anyone could be so cruel – and at Christmas too!" He thought for a moment. "I'll take them down to the Dogs' Home," he decided. "They never close. If I cut through the back streets, I'll only be a couple of minutes. Though I'm not sure if anyone can help the poor creatures now."

Kibby's eyes filled with tears. "You mean they're all going to *die?*" she asked, her lower lip beginning to quiver. "Can't we save them?"

"Probably not. Cover for me at home," Zan instructed. "I won't be long." He carefully picked up the sack, and, with Jenna bounding at his heels, he skated off down the icy slope towards the road.

◆

Kibby met up with her brother again some twenty minutes later at the end of Tin Can Alley. It was pitch dark and bitterly cold. A sharp ground frost was spreading carpets of diamonds underneath the street lights.

"Mum wants you inside now," she warned. "How did it go?"

"I put the sack on the top step and rang the bell. Then I hid. I saw someone take it inside."

"Why did you hide?" asked Kibby curiously. Then she heard a frantic whimpering coming from inside Zan's jacket. He pulled it aside gently to reveal a tiny brown puppy huddled against his jersey. It began to tremble violently in the night air, so Zan quickly covered it up again.

"You *took* one?" said Kibby in amazement.

"Yes, he was the strongest. He perked right up as soon as he felt some warmth. I just know he's going to live, so I've decided to keep him."

"Keep him? But where? Mum will go crazy!"

"She doesn't need to know, does she? It'll be our secret, Kibs. I'm going to make a bed for him under my bunk. He's so tiny, he'll barely eat a thing, and he'll only drink milk at first anyway. I can save my newspaper-round money for biscuits, and if I let Toby Powers share my computer, then he can pay me back with meat scraps from his Dad's shop. He'd do anything to use it."

"Well, you seem to have thought of *everything*," said Kibby with admiration. "I'm proud of you, Zan!"

"Thanks. Secret Mission, then, sis?"

"Secret!" the little girl confirmed, and the two gave their special handshake and ended with a high five.

"Well, that's all fixed, then!" declared Zan with a satisfied grin. "It'll be such fun. What can possibly go wrong?"

CHAPTER THREE

The following weekend, a brief article appeared on page five of the weekly *Sunfield Satellite*. It told of an abandoned litter of puppies which had found its way onto the doorstep of the local Dogs' Home. The staff had done everything they could, but, sadly, there had been no survivors.

Mr. Makepeace was busy mending the old shed door that weekend, and he did not study the newspaper closely. Mrs. Makepeace only skimmed quickly through the headlines on each page, so she missed the article too. On Monday morning Zan stood his shoes on page five while he cleaned them, and in the afternoon Kibby tore it up into jigsaw pieces to complete a papier-mâché stable she was making from an old shoe box. She pasted the pieces carefully over the roof and painted them dark brown.

One young woman did not miss the article — in fact, she went out of her way to find it. She went over it again and again, and at last she picked up some scissors, cut out the small passage neatly, and stuck it proudly onto page one of a new scrapbook. She hoped there would be plenty more pieces to follow.

The young woman's name was Tansy Briar. She was a journalist, and this article was her first in her new job on the *Sunfield Satellite.* She could hardly wait to show it to her close friend Matthew Harding, who worked as a biologist at Rowan Park Wild Animal Sanctuary, miles away on the other side of London.

◆

Zan and Kibby willed the tiny pup back to life; it just *had* to survive! Little did either of them know how close to death the abandoned creature had come. However, tucked snugly in an old jersey against the piece of radiator under Zan's bunk, it rested, and grew warm at last. Zan had propped a bottle of milk against the radiator too, so it was always tepid and ready to use, and Kibby had found an old medicine dropper in the bathroom cabinet, which was perfect for feeding their fragile patient.

At first, the precious drops of warm milk dripped everywhere, all down the pup's bare chin and onto its skinny stomach. It blew milky bubbles and snuffled and wheezed for breath, desperately trying to swallow at the same time. It made such a mess that Zan half expected the milk to start coming out of its ears too! Slowly, very slowly, the little creature learnt to drink from the dropper, growing more expert and more eager with every feeding. Finally, one day it grasped the dropper in both tiny brown paws and began to suck noisily, drinking the entire contents and then whimpering excitedly for more. From that memorable moment onwards, the pup began to grow strong. It had won the battle for life!

◆

Zan was all smiles at supper, as he polished off his meal in record time. Mr. and Mrs. Makepeace thought it was wonderful to have their son in such good spirits at last. He was happy and willing to help with anything, and he and Kibby seemed the very best of friends. Gone was the sulky, resentful boy of the previous year.

"What an excellent idea those in-line skates were!" Zan's parents had agreed.

When he had eaten the last of his apple crumble, Zan pushed back his chair and gave a satisfied sigh. "That was marvellous, Mum!" he beamed at her. "I've been meaning to tell you, I've made a special New Year's resolution."

"Do tell," encouraged Sam Makepeace, with a sly wink at Kibby. "What is it this year?"

"I've decided that from now on, I'm going to clean and tidy my bedroom myself," Zan announced firmly. "I promise it'll be spotless, Mum, so there won't be anything at all for you to do. In fact, you needn't even go in there any more, if you don't want to!"

Mrs. Makepeace was surprised and delighted. Zan was showing the first signs of really growing up at last.

"Thank you dear," she said. "Nothing would make me happier." For Zan's room had always looked as though a tornado had just passed through it.

His father patted him on the back. "Well done, son!" Then, because none of them wanted to tempt fate any further, the matter came peacefully to rest.

◆

"How's old Stinky today, then?" chirped Kibby as she bounced into Zan's bedroom. "Stinky? Where are you?" She closed the door behind her, leaving the DO NOT DISTURB! sign, which their parents had thought so amusing, swinging from the doorknob outside.

"Don't call him stupid names!" Zan reprimanded. "And he doesn't smell any more!" The pup's wriggling warmth felt wonderful in his arms.

"Well, we'd better think of a new name for him," Kibby retorted. She looked at the patches of dark fur which were growing into a lopsided mask around the pup's eyes. "How about Bandit?"

Zan considered it. "Bandit's not bad," he told his sister. "But he's far too friendly for that." He traced his finger round the soft tufts of hair which were now starting to grow thickly all over the puppy's body. "Just like little swirls of smoke," he mused. Then he cried, "*That's* it, Kib! He's starting to look just like a tiny puff of grey smoke, so that's what I'll call him – Smoke!" He paused. "Here, Smoke!"

The puppy blinked half-opened eyes at him and gave a little whimper.

"There you are!" Zan exclaimed triumphantly. "He knows his name already!"

◆

Slowly, Smoke began to grow. At first it was hard to detect any difference day by day, but after a week Zan and Kibby could easily see the progress he had made.

Zan carefully measured the pup from the end of his rubbery grey nose to the quivering tip of his stubby tail. "Two more centimetres! Well done, boy!"

Smoke blinked at the sound of Zan's voice and whined with pleasure. He knew it was nearly time for some more milk.

"He's going to be an incredibly handsome chap," Zan remarked, as proudly as a doting father. And indeed it was obvious that Smoke, who had so recently been such a fragile waif, was changing into an impressive creature.

Obtaining enough milk for him to drink was no problem at all. This was just as well, for Smoke's thirst was never sated. Once he discovered how to feed from the dropper, he drank so much that his stomach sometimes swelled as though he had swallowed a tennis ball, and Zan feared that one day he might actually burst!

The boy rode an early morning paper round in a wide

circle around Sunfield. He always met Mr. Bailey, the milkman, somewhere along the way. Often he bought a pint of milk, but sometimes the friendly milkman would hand him any leftovers on his way back to the depot.

"Now *that's* what I like to see!" he told the boy cheerfully. "Nothing healthier for a growing lad than a nice fresh pint of milk! Certainly beats all the fizzy pop you kids drink nowadays!"

Zan would thank him, take a hasty swig, and wipe his milky moustache. Then, as soon as Mr. Bailey was out of sight, he would hide the bottle away in his saddlebag.

Deceiving his parents was easy. With Zan's mother working until past three-thirty in the afternoons, and his father safely asleep upstairs, it was no trouble for the boy to slip out of school during lunch break, cycle home, and sneak in through his bedroom window to spend precious extra minutes with his puppy.

After two weeks, young Smoke was finally on his feet, trotting bravely about the room on sturdy little legs.

The bedroom floor was linoleum, making it easy to wash, but its shiny surface made for a very slippery foothold. Smoke delighted in exploring every inch of what must have seemed like the biggest den in the world. Anything that moved, from flies to ping pong balls, *had* to be investigated. North, south, east, and west were easy, but up and down had to be learnt the hard way! However heavily he tumbled, though, his fluffy tail never stopped wagging. And as soon as Zan lifted him into his arms, the pup was yelping and wriggling with pleasure, and covering the boy's face with warm, wet licks.

Smoke was everything a boy could wish for, and Zan loved the pup with all his heart. He had never been happier.

CHAPTER FOUR

 By late February, Smoke was two months old, and he was becoming a real little terror! His one saving grace was that he rarely barked, although Zan and Kibby knew he had a voice. For he whined and whimpered ecstatically, rolling over on his back to be petted, whenever either of them entered the room.

Zan seemed to spend his life mopping up Atlantic-sized puddles from the bedroom floor, and thanking his lucky stars there was no carpet. This was one problem he had not considered in advance, but somehow, between them, he and Kibby managed to keep the situation reasonably under control.

Smoke learned very early on that anyone except for Zan and Kibby was the enemy. He instinctively dived for cover and froze whenever he heard approaching footsteps. His bed under Zan's bunk was the safest place he knew, and it was there that he bolted if any stranger came into the bedroom.

For Zan and Kibby this was ideal, for it gave them both plenty of time to assume stage positions of total involvement in something else – Zan at his computer and Kibby sprawled on the bed with her nose in a pony book.

Mrs. Makepeace had no complaints, though. Occasionally she thought she heard rather a lot of scuffling as she crossed the hall, and maybe Zan's bedroom did not look quite as spotless as she would have liked. Sometimes she thought she could detect a faint hint of a strange animal smell, masked by a pine disinfectant. Zan had protested that it was his new bath talc. However, she put it down to unwashed socks in the laundry basket, or perhaps those smelly old trainers that her son wore constantly. They had certainly seen better days, but new ones were so expensive.

Before long, the bedroom, which had at first seemed enormous to Smoke, had begun to diminish in size. It was as though the walls were slowly closing in on him. Two months of age was a major turning point for such an energetic little creature. Almost before Zan knew it, the time had come for two very big changes in the young pup's life.

The first was his diet. Milk was no longer enough for him. For a short while, Zan and Kibby smuggled sweet biscuits and cereal from the kitchen and tiny pieces of cooked meat off their supper plates, which he wolfed down with delight. Once Zan bought him a tin of dog food to try, but Smoke refused to eat it.

There was nothing else for it – Toby Powers, the butcher's son, had to be sworn into the pact.

Smoke and Toby met for the first time on a Sunday afternoon in late February, and it was not an enormous success. At the sight of a stranger, Smoke gave a yelp of fright and dived under the bed, refusing to come out until the newcomer had left. However, Toby had just managed to catch a glimpse of him.

"What a strange-looking dog," he remarked. "I like his yellow eyes!" For Smoke's eyes, which had been pale blue at birth, had gradually turned "the colour of melted butter," as Kibby had observed, and in the darkness, or whenever they caught the glint of an artificial light, they shone with a luminous gleam.

"He's not a strange-looking dog!" Zan protested loyally. "He's a German shepherd – you'll see, when he's grown a little more."

"Nah," said Toby, "my uncle's got one of those. Your pup looks more like the huskies I saw on TV the other night. They were pulling a sled through the snow."

"Yes, I saw them too," said Kibby. "And he's right, Zan, Smoke *does* look a little like a sled-dog."

Zan hesitated, confused. "Well, maybe he's a cross-breed, then," he said grudgingly. "So he must be a German husky."

And, as they were all happy with that explanation, a "German husky" is what Smoke became.

Toby Powers was a pleasant, trustworthy boy. He was so thrilled to finally be allowed to use Zan's computer that he would have agreed to anything as a favour in return.

"It won't be a problem," he assured Zan. "Dad keeps a big section in one freezer for all the odds and ends. He supplies offal to the Dogs' Home and lots of other places. I'll bring over a bag of meat whenever I come to use the computer." His eyes shone with anticipation.

"What's offal?" Kibby asked.

"Innards!" Toby told her with relish. "Blood and guts, and entrails!" He pulled a gruesome face at her.

"How awful!" she sniffed delicately.

"How *offal!*" Toby teased, and began to giggle.

"Smoke's so tiny he'll hardly eat a thing," Zan assured his new friend. "And I'll come in and buy mince whenever I can afford it. I can always say it's a treat for Jenna. I can use her as a red herring."

"A red herring?" Kibby piped up again. "Will Smoke eat fish too?" She looked hurt when both boys burst into shrieks of laughter.

"Hey, Kibby, red herrings on toast for your tea?"

"Shut up, you pig. I hate you!"

"Leave her alone, Tobes. She's a little hard of herring!"

◆

The second major change in Smoke's young life was that he must now venture into the great outdoors. Zan had often found him sitting on the bed, ears cocked with curiosity as he stared out of the window. The moment had arrived to take him outside and let him roam, as all pups should.

One day after school, when Toby was installed at the computer, Zan fetched his bicycle from the shed and leant it up against the wall underneath his window. The saddle-bag was large and roomy, and it was easy to pop the wriggling pup in and strap him safely inside.

Then the boy rode carefully down the alley, with Kibby running along behind, until he reached the waste ground at the far end.

After fastening an old leather strap around the pup's neck, Zan attached a ball of strong white string to it. Then, for the very first time, Smoke's soft grey pads touched the earth and he was free! Well, free for as far as he could reach on the end of his string. But, to the tiny pup, this seemed to be to the edge of the earth.

Smoke had always been cautious about anything new, but now curiosity took over. Before long, he was rolling and bouncing about in the grass as though he were completely mad. He seemed almost drunk with the smell of the fresh air and the heady new experience of stretching his stubby legs and running. He frequently stumbled and tripped, as Zan had done with his new in-line skates. But gradually he found his footing on the rough ground and quickly learned to move with more agility.

Then, suddenly, he was worn out. He flopped down just where he was, in a big patch of mud, closed his eyes, and went to sleep.

Zan and Kibby rushed over, frantic with concern, but their worries proved unfounded. One bleary eye opened, and a small tail cranked stiffly into life again.

"He's not hurt at all," Zan assured his sister. He smiled as he gently gathered up the limp, muddy little body. "It's just that his batteries have run out!" Like two devoted parents, they carried the exhausted pup slowly home to bed.

◆

February gave way to March, and Smoke continued to grow. Soon, even Zan was starting to worry about just how big he would finally be. For the tiny, fragile pup was turning into a strong animal, with a thick, smoky-grey overcoat. His eyes had deepened to an even more beautiful shade of liquid amber.

Jenna soon became wise to the exercise routines, and, although she had been a little jealous of the new arrival at first, the stray collie's maternal instincts quickly took over.

When Smoke was small, Jenna had played very gently with him, rolling him around in the grass and licking him tenderly should he ever seem to be hurt. But now, at three months, he was bigger than Jenna, and the two played as equals. And Smoke kept growing.

◆

Three months later, on a glorious June afternoon, Zan and Toby stretched out idly on the grass of the waste ground to watch Smoke and Jenna's exuberant games. The heat of the late afternoon sunshine was paradise! A day like this was too good to waste indoors on the computer.

Behind them, fragrant banks of brilliant pink rosebay willow herb were buzzing with clouds of honey bees. Dotted across the waste ground, scrubby growths of the invasive but beautiful purple buddleia lived up to its other name – the butterfly bush. The afternoon haze was alive with red admiral and peacock butterflies, fluttering in their dozens above the boys' heads like multi-coloured jewels, on an endless search for nectar. They were joined by armies of hoverflies, and all manner of other flying insects. It was an entomologist's dream. Even in the city, midsummer days could be magic.

"I can't believe how big Smoke has grown!" Zan remarked. "With the amount of meat he's eating now, I'm not surprised!" Toby replied. "Pretty soon, he'll be the size of a wolf!"

"I'm sorry." Zan felt obliged to apologise. "I'll find a holiday job as soon as school breaks up, then I'll be able to afford more food myself." He paused. "I'm so grateful, Toby. I couldn't have managed without you."

Toby smiled at his friend. He knew how much Smoke meant to him. "It's all right," he said generously. "Smoke's a fine dog, and I admire the way you saved his life."

Zan could hardly wait for the last few days of school to be over. The holidays would give him much more time to spend outside with Smoke, now that the weather was so good.

It was a small miracle that he and Kibby, and of course Toby, had managed to keep their secret safe for so long.

But during the school holidays there would be dangerous times when Smoke might be found out. Inevitably, the long mid-summer days were sure to bring many new tests for them all.

◆

By five o'clock, the dusty city was shimmering in the heat-haze. Miles away, on the other side of London, Rowan Park Wild Animal Sanctuary slumbered peacefully, free from the bustle of visitors at last.

A female voice broke through the stillness. "Elsa! Sheba! Come on, girls! Tea-time!" Near one of the largest enclosures, Caroline, the keeper, deposited a small carcass on the ground, then went back through the gate, fastening the bolts securely behind her. She stood for a moment or two, scanning the silent woods. But they remained deserted.

"Come on, girls, before the magpies get it!" she urged. Then she turned and strolled away down the path.

Deep in the cool of a patch of dense woodland, two sets of amber eyes blinked as they watched her departure. And two noses twitched enthusiastically at the smell of food which wafted towards them on the breeze. But despite their hunger, the nervous creatures waited several minutes more, until the young woman had vanished completely from sight, before slinking cautiously down to feed.

CHAPTER FIVE

Mrs. Makepeace smiled when she spotted the DO NOT DISTURB! sign hanging on her son's doorknob. It was a Saturday in June, and Zan had gone shopping with Kibby and his father, but he had forgotten to leave out his dirty washing. This created a good excuse for his mother to venture into the forbidden territory of Zan's room, just to make sure the housework was up to scratch.

As she entered, June Makepeace noticed that the room was neat, and fairly clean. Well, as clean as could be expected for a twelve-year-old boy! But there was still a peculiar smell in the air, even though the window was open wide. Was it the bedside mat? Old shoes? Dog? She could not define it.

Zan had a treasured natural history collection on his shelves. It comprised bits of wood, some fossilised chalk, seaweed from a holiday in Devon, and a very moth-eaten stuffed bird of prey which he had brought home with glee from the local flea market. Mrs. Makepeace decided it must be the bird. She sniffed. Horrible! If she had her way, it would be out with the rubbish by Monday!

She collected the washing, then tugged at the bedside mat. It certainly needed cleaning too. For a moment, the mat would not come out. It felt heavy, as though something was standing on it. Then, as she bent down to look, suddenly it pulled free, and she almost toppled over. There was a piece of bone lying at her feet. She picked it up, smiling to herself again, and put it carefully on Zan's desk. "I bet he thinks it's a dinosaur's kneebone!" she mused.

Then Mrs. Makepeace noticed the wall beneath the open window, and the white-painted sill itself. They were both grey with dirt, covered with smears and splodges and earthy scuffs, some of which looked like paw marks.

"Oh, Zan," she sighed. "If only you would stop climbing out of the window. It's just a few steps through the kitchen to the back door. But I suppose boys will be boys!"

She fetched a bucket filled with hot water and lemon-scented detergent, and soon its pungent odour had permeated the room. As she knelt down beside the bed to scrub the dirty wall, she thought she heard a stifled sneeze behind her. Her imagination must be playing tricks. Maybe it was the ghost of that wretched bird, come back to haunt her!

Her ankle and shoe stretched out underneath the bunk as she worked. Very slowly, a grey nose drew nearer and nearer, paused an inch or two away, and sniffed them cautiously. Mrs. Makepeace began to hum as she worked, and a pair of ears cocked at the strange new sound. Two amber eyes blinked silently in the half-light, as they followed her every move.

◆

The next close shave occurred one morning just after the school holidays had started, when Mrs. Makepeace had left early for work. As their father was not due home for at least an hour, Zan and Kibby had allowed Smoke out into the kitchen for the first time.

Soon the two children were sitting at the pine table, laughing and chatting, and feeding the pup pieces of toast and black cherry jam. Suddenly, Smoke's ears pricked up, and he gave a single sharp bark. Zan glanced through the window and saw his father coming up the garden path. He leapt to his feet. There was no time to smuggle Smoke back to the bedroom.

"Go and meet Dad on the doorstep, Kib! *Quickly!*" he cried. "Delay him for as long as you can, or we're done for! If he sees Smoke, he'll make giblets out of us!"

By the time Kibby and Mr. Makepeace came into the kitchen, Zan was sitting alone at the table, innocently munching his toast.

"Where is he?" Kibby mouthed.

Zan indicated the larder, and Kibby stifled a giggle. The larder was tiny, and crammed full of everything imaginable. There was barely room inside for a mouse, let alone a creature of Smoke's size.

Mr. Makepeace sat down at the table and sighed heavily. "What a night!" he exclaimed. "I'm starving. What's for breakfast today, then?" He slowly rose to his feet again and headed for the larder. "Is there any cereal left?" he asked. Zan bounded over to the larder door and stood in front of his father. "Do sit down, Dad," he coaxed. "You've had such a hard night's work, why don't we wait on you for a change?"

"Well, that sounds like a fine idea, son!" Mr. Makepeace enthused, sitting down again at the table.

At that moment, there was a tremendous crash from the larder, followed by some odd snuffling and crunching noises.

"Oh no!" cried Kibby, jumping up anxiously. "The Oatie Crunch must have fallen onto the floor!" She ran to the larder and peeped inside. "I can't have pushed it properly back onto the shelf. What a mess!"

The cereal packet lay on the red tiles. Smoke was busy polishing off the last few grains.

Zan chipped in with a hasty smile, "Sorry, Dad. Will you have poached eggs on toast instead?"

"Don't worry, Dad," said Kibby sweetly. "I'll sweep up later." She turned away to hide another attack of the giggles, while her brother rummaged noisily in the cupboard to find a saucepan. Mr. Makepeace laughed heartily, enjoying the good-natured banter.

He seemed to take hours to eat his breakfast, but at last every morsel was gone and he pushed back his chair.

"That was excellent," he complimented the children, smothering a yawn. "Now I think I'll have a shower and go up to bed. What luxury – I could get used to this!"

There was a muffled snort.

"Was that you, Kibby?" Mr. Makepeace asked, turning in surprise. "Not coming down with a summer cold, are you?"

"Oh – er – no," the girl stammered. "Just a tickle, I think." She gave a very unconvincing sneeze. "I'll start sweeping the larder."

Zan clattered the dishes in the sink until his father had finally left the room.

The children both burst into laughter and rushed over to the larder. Smoke had finished the whole box of Oatie Crunch, devoured a large bag of cheese and onion crisps, and broken a jar of marmalade. Then he had moved on to a giant-sized packet of chocolate biscuits. The floor was covered with a sticky mixture of crumbs and marmalade, blended with some brown shoe polish which he had knocked off the bottom shelf. Smoke himself was looking rather queasy. Evidently, he had eaten too much.

Zan gave a howl of dismay. "Oh, *no!* Stop laughing, Kibbles, this is a catastrophe! It'll take *ages* to clear up. Quick, let's put old greedy-guts back in my room. Oh, you *are* a bad dog! There'll be no supper for *you* tonight!"

"He's got shoe polish all over his feet!" Kibby gurgled.

"He looks like a yeti! Mum'll go mad – the carpet will be ruined."

"Well, we'll just have to carry him, then," said Zan. But Smoke was, by now, far too heavy for even the two of them to lift.

"Let's tie some dish cloths round his paws," suggested Zan in desperation. "Then you start cleaning, while I go down to the corner store to buy more of everything. It's going to cost me a small fortune!"

Smoke was still licking the marmalade off his muzzle as he looked cheerfully at Zan and Kibby. He wagged his tail gently. His day was certainly off to an excellent start!

It took most of the morning to tidy up the mess, but by the time Mrs. Makepeace arrived home for lunch she found the kitchen spic and span.

"We've even cleared out the larder for you, Mum!" crowed Kibby, giving her mother an angelic smile. "It was an extra holiday job, so will there be extra pocket money on Saturday?"

Zan elbowed Kibby in the ribs. She was really pushing her luck!

Thankfully, Smoke was still a strangely quiet creature. He rarely barked, and made only the smallest of yelping and whimpering noises of welcome whenever Zan or Kibby came into the room. Tail tucked between his legs, he would whine and cower submissively until they bent down to pet him, whereupon, grinning with pleasure, he would lick their faces and sniff carefully round their mouths and ears. Zan always made a point of sniffing Smoke's ears in return – it seemed to make him feel more secure.

"Goodness, Smoke, don't cower so," the boy would tell him. "Anyone would think we beat you, instead of giving you all this pampering!"

One Friday evening, Mr. and Mrs. Makepeace had gone into the city. It was their fifteenth wedding anniversary, and Sam Makepeace had surprised his wife with a rare dinner date and tickets for a West End show.

With a promise from the next-door neighbours to keep a watchful eye on them, Zan and Kibby had been left with the house to themselves for a whole marvellous evening. As soon as the coast was finally clear, Zan opened his bedroom door.

Smoke tiptoed cautiously into the house, and the two children watched in anticipation as their beloved pet wandered round, sniffing every nook and cranny, his elegant plumed tail wagging gently with pleasure. When at last he had investigated every inch of each room, he came back and lay down on the rug at Zan's feet, chin on paws, to relax. Zan stroked his soft head triumphantly.

"Just like a proper dog," he remarked to his sister, his eyes sparkling with pride. "Wouldn't it be wonderful if he could do this all the time?"

"Maybe one day, Zan. Maybe Mum will let him."

"In our dreams, Kib."

When the novelty of Smoke's freedom had begun to

wear off a little, Kibby switched on the television. The first programme was an opera. Zan thought opera a very strange form of entertainment. And it was far too loud.

"Ouch, what a racket!" he winced, turning down the sound. "Listen Kibby! Cats – lots of cats!" He howled, mimicking the soprano. "Owoooooo!"

"Idiot!" Kibby giggled, her mouth full of chocolate. "You sound like a werewolf!"

Smoke, who was watching Zan intently, suddenly drew a deep breath. Then, stretching his nose high into the air, he began to make the most extraordinary noise.

It started off as a rumble, very low in his throat. Gradually it built in volume, becoming louder and higher by the second, until the entire room was filled with a weird and ghostly yowl. It completely drowned out the voice of the opera singer and made the hairs stand up on the back of Zan's and Kibby's necks.

"Kibs, listen to that! He's howling like a wolf!"

The two children looked at each other, open-mouthed. Then Kibby gave a shout of delight. "He's singing, Zan, Smoke's singing!"

Zan howled again. "Owoooooo . . . ." And the more he howled, the more Smoke howled too, until the sound echoed along the corridors, as though the house was filled with a thousand wailing banshees. "Yowwoooo . . . ."

"You'd better stop!" Kibby shrieked frantically. "Or Mr. and Mrs. Kelly will be round from next door to find out what on earth's going on in here!"

Zan stared at Smoke in astonishment. "Would you believe it, Kibs?" he exclaimed, as he smoothed down the hair along his pup's shaggy back. "A singing dog. A real, live singing dog! Smoke seems to bring us more surprises with every single day. And I don't suppose he's finished *yet!*"

CHAPTER SIX

 By July, people were beginning to complain about the heat. But for Zan and Smoke, life could not have been more perfect.

At a quarter to six each morning, the boy would set off on his newspaper round, with Smoke loping eagerly along beside the bicycle. Every day, the animal's legs seemed to grow a little longer, and every day he ran a little faster. He was a lithe and agile creature now, and striking to behold. Usually, he lay panting in the shade during the hottest hours of the day. But at dawn and dusk, he really seemed to come alive.

For the first summer he could remember, Zan was not lonely. Now he had a constant companion, a best friend, and a soul-mate all wrapped up into one, and he was altogether a different person.

The boy and his beloved pet had become a familiar sight in the neighbourhood.

"Morning, Zan!" tradesmen called briskly as they passed by.

"Morning, young Smoke!" Old Mr. Blakeney would cheerfully wave his carved walking stick as he strolled along on his early morning circuit of the streets. "Gorgeous day again!"

The air was filled with a chorus of birdsong at this early hour. The ancient lime trees which lined the avenues provided a fleeting moment's shade. And Zan could hear a symphony of crickets among the sun-dried grasses on a patchwork of waste ground along the roadside.

◆

June Makepeace literally bumped into old Mr. Blakeney outside the newsagent's shop one lunchtime.

"Hello there!" he said. "I always see that fine young lad of yours out on his early morning rounds. My goodness, how that pup of his has grown. What a handsome creature Smoke is!"

Mrs. Makepeace looked a little puzzled. "A pup? Zan has a *dog* with him?" she said. Then she laughed. "Oh, you must mean Jenna! Dear me, Zan and his strays. Jenna's a nice little collie really, but of course I could never have her inside the house with all those fleas, no matter how hard Zan begs me!"

"A *collie?*" It was Mr. Blakeney's turn to look puzzled. "I don't know much about dogs, but I don't think that magnificent pup was a *collie*. And I could have sworn Zan said his name was Smoke!"

As he spoke, an enormous lorry thundered past, the

choking backdraft almost knocking them both right off the pavement. The noise drowned out most of Tom Blakeney's sentence, and the only word Mrs. Makepeace caught clearly was "smoke." She assumed he was referring to the lorry.

"What a monster – awful, isn't it?" she remarked, smiling vaguely at her confused companion. "We really need that new by-pass, don't we?" Then she wished him a good day and set off for home.

◆

The instant Zan opened his bedroom door, he knew something was wrong. The window was open far wider than usual, and his computer chair lay overturned on the floor. There was tension in the air.

"Toby, is that you?" he asked cautiously, but there was no reply. Walking across to his desk, Zan put down the sandwich he was holding, picked up the chair, and pushed it back into place.

"Smoke?" he said. "Where are you, boy?"

Quite often nowadays, Smoke was allowed outside by himself. He needed so much exercise, it seemed kinder to leave the window open for him so that he could come and go as he pleased. He never went far, just to meet up with Jenna and the rest of the alley pack on the waste ground. There, under Thor's guidance, the stray dogs educated him, treating the growing pup like one of their own. Soon Smoke could take good care of himself. He had learnt very quickly to be street-wise – to elude the catchers from the Dogs' Home, out on patrol with their evil-looking nooses.

"Under the bed!" A fear-filled voice made Zan jump. He spun round to see a teenage lad, probably a year or two older than himself, pressed up against the wall in the back corner of the room.

"It's under the bed!" the lad exclaimed again. His jacket was torn and filthy, and his jet-black hair made his terrified face appear even whiter.

Smoke edged out of his lair on his stomach and looked up expectantly at Zan. The tip of his tail tapped the ground faintly in welcome.

Zan stared in amazement from Smoke to the lad and back again. For a moment or two no one uttered a sound. It was hard to decide who was more frightened – the intruder or Smoke.

They both looked so funny that Zan began to laugh. "Smoke wouldn't have hurt you!" he told the lad, fondling the pup's ears.

Smoke's tail began to wag a little harder. Help was on hand!

"He wouldn't harm a flea! He's really as soft as butter. A fine old guard dog, eh?"

"But he looks so fierce!" the lad said. "I thought he'd eat me alive for sure!" Slowly he crept out of the corner, still trembling, but straightening his jacket in an attempt to look less foolish.

"What are you doing in my room anyway?" Zan

demanded, keen to step in while he still had the upper hand.

The intruder hesitated. "The computer," he said finally. "I only came in to look at it. The window was open. I wouldn't have taken anything – honest!"

Zan stared hard at him. Honest? He didn't look very honest. Was he telling the truth or not? There was another awkward pause.

"It's a real beauty, isn't it?" the lad said enviously. Then, "I'm Jacob – my mates call me Jake. Pleased to meet you." He wiped a grimy hand down his jeans and held it out formally.

His palm felt clammy in Zan's grasp. "I won it," Zan told him, beginning to warm a little to his unexpected visitor. "I'm Zan, and this is my dog, Smoke. I raised him from a newborn pup." He shook hands with Jake.

By now the lad was eyeing the large cheese and pickle sandwich which beckoned temptingly from the desk.

"Are you hungry? D'you want it?" Zan enquired. "Go ahead – help yourself!"

Jake ate the sandwich in a few huge mouthfuls, rather as Jenna might have done. As though he had not eaten for days. Then, edging warily round Smoke's recumbent form, he scrambled hastily out of the window. He said just one more word before vanishing as mysteriously as he had come: a gruff and ungracious "Thanks!"

◆

By mid-August, the sun was really beginning to scorch the ground. The wayside grasses were parched yellow with drought, and the air tasted bitter with city dust.

Mrs. Makepeace had even encouraged Zan to take a washing-up bowl filled with water out to the waste ground for Jenna and the alley pack dogs.

"Poor things," she said, "they'd be far better off in that Home."

"No, they wouldn't!" Zan had rushed to their defence. "They're fine, Mum – really they are. Surely it's far better to be free."

His mother sighed. "Perhaps, but it's not much of a life to be homeless. Reduced to wandering the streets day after day. Always searching for the next meal and somewhere safe to sleep for the night. It's certainly not my idea of freedom."

Zan shrugged. He had no answer for her.

◆

Life in Sunfield crawled along at a virtual standstill. Whenever possible, folk stayed inside. Weary commuters clustered under the sprawling elm trees in the parks, eager for a moment's respite from the scalding sun, before continuing their sticky journeys. The brown lawns were empty. Only the most foolhardy continued to sunbathe in the midday heat.

On August seventeenth, something happened in the Makepeace household which was to change all of their lives forever.

The afternoon had started off ordinarily enough. Zan and Kibby were with Smoke in Zan's room. They had opened the window wide so that the sultry air could circulate. Zan was seated at his computer, trying to master a particularly complicated new game, while his sister groomed Smoke's glorious summer coat. All was quiet, and deceptively peaceful.

"You poor old thing, Smokey," Kibby had sympathized. "How you must be suffering!"

It was true. Smoke did not enjoy such intense heat at all. He panted constantly and lapped frequently from his water bowl. Outside, he relished the children's water fights with the garden hose, rolling in the jet until he was soaked through.

Kibby was lying on the floor, where the lino felt cool on her bare legs. Lazily she reached out a hand to tickle Smoke's soft, white stomach. Heat wave or no, he adored this luxury. Obligingly, he rolled over, flat on his back with all four feet in the air. He looked as endearing as the tiny pup he had once been. Stretching to full length and spreading out his toes, Smoke gave a giant-sized yawn.

He must have heard the approaching footsteps before Zan and Kibby did. But perhaps he was just too warm, and too distracted by pleasure, to care. By the time Zan heard his mother coming across the hallway, it was too late.

"Quick, Smoke, SCRAM!" the boy cried out, frantically clapping his hands. But Smoke didn't.

"Zan? Is Kibby with you?" Mrs. Makepeace turned the doorknob and walked into the room.

Her bright smile of greeting froze into an expression of pure horror as her eyes met Smoke's yellow glare.

CHAPTER SEVEN

Suddenly there was pandemonium. Kibby gave a frightened little cry, leapt up, and overturned the bedside table. Zan jumped to his feet too, and grabbed Smoke, trying hard to shield him from sight. But this time Smoke did not dive under the bed, nor did he freeze with fright. Now he was old enough to stand his ground. Eyes flashing, he bared his teeth in a snarl.

It was all bluff, but to Mrs. Makepeace he looked truly awesome. She gave a shriek and stepped backwards into the doorway, almost knocking over her husband, who had just appeared to see what all the noise was about.

"What on earth . . . ?" he began sleepily, totally confused.

"Come out! Come out!" June Makepeace cried urgently to Kibby. "What is this monstrous creature doing in here, Zan?"

"He's *not* a monster!" Zan shouted back defiantly. "He's Smoke, and he's my dog!"

"So you *did* take in a stray dog after all? *That's* what's been going on. Oh, you wicked, disobedient boy!" his mother wailed hysterically. "How could you put your little sister in such danger? That wretched creature looks completely mad! It might have rabies!"

"Oh, don't be so stupid, mother!" Zan shouted back. "Anyone can see he's in the peak of health!"

"How *dare* you talk to your mother like that!" Sam Makepeace's voice thundered above the mêlée.

Mrs. Makepeace grabbed Kibby's arm and began to pull her towards the door. "Come out this moment, before you're bitten. We'll all be savaged!"

"No, we *won't!*" Kibby shouted, beginning to cry. "Smokey's as gentle as a kitten, really he is, Mum."

Smoke was terrified. For the first time in his life, his "family" faced real danger – surely this was the enemy the alley pack had taught him about. All he could think of was protecting Kibby. Despite his own fear, he leapt forward, snarling like a demon, grabbed hold of her shirt in his huge teeth, and tugged her away from Mrs. Makepeace as hard as he could.

Everyone was screaming and shouting again. Zan's computer keyboard crashed to the floor as he leapt forward, shook Smoke by the scruff of the neck, and yelled, "Drop her, Smoke! Let her go!"

Smoke did as he was told.

Sam Makepeace pushed his wife and daughter out of the room. Then, taking Zan's arm, he propelled him

through the doorway too. He slammed the bedroom door shut.

Inside, Smoke was still pacing back and forth, snarling with anger and fear.

White and trembling, the whole family stood in the hallway. Mr. Makepeace rounded on his son. "Have you gone completely insane, boy?" he roared. "What do you think you're doing, keeping that vicious creature in there? How long has this been going on?"

By now, June Makepeace was beginning to calm down a little. "Zan, these street dogs are semi-wild," she reproached him. "You and Kibby could have been seriously hurt."

"Smoke's as tame as anything," Zan said heatedly. "We saved his life. He loves us!"

"I've never heard such nonsense!" Sam Makepeace was beginning to raise his voice again. "I shall telephone the Dogs' Home straight away. They must come and remove the animal!"

Zan went whiter still. "Oh, please, *no*, Dad!" he shouted. "NO!"

But his protests were in vain. Mr. Makepeace locked the bedroom door and pocketed the key. "No one is to go in there until the experts arrive," he said grimly, and there was nothing either Zan or Kibby could say to change his mind.

Mrs. Makepeace hurried off to the kitchen to make some tea, and the two children sat down together on the sofa in shocked silence.

◆

When Pete Barker arrived from the Dogs' Home, he carried a white wire cage in one hand and a long pole with a noose on the end in the other. Zan shuddered.

Kibby had one final try. "He's our pet, Mr. Barker," she cried out loyally, "and he wouldn't hurt a *fly*. Oh, *please*, Mum, let Zan keep him!"

"The dog's half-mad," said Mr. Makepeace brusquely. "You saw how it tried to attack you. It's totally out of the question, Kathlyn. I've never heard such insanity!"

Pete Barker was feeling rather uncomfortable, for Zan had worked hard at the Dogs' Home on many occasions. "Let's shed some light on the subject," he said as kindly as he could. He cautiously opened the bedroom door and peeped around it.

Then he stopped dead, closed the door again quickly, and gave an audible gulp. "Oh, my goodness!" he said. "If I hadn't seen it with my own eyes, I would never have believed it possible!"

"Can you take the dog?" Mr. Makepeace broke in impatiently.

"Well, sir, that's just the problem." Pete's eyes were bulging with fright. "It isn't a *dog* at all. It's a *wolf!* A Canadian timber wolf, almost full-grown!"

There was a brief silence. Then everyone began to talk at once.

"He's *not* a *wolf*. Tell them, Zan!"

"Smoke's a *German husky!*"

"Oh, my saints! We could all have been killed and eaten!"

"Remove that deranged creature from my house at once! Lock it up, shoot it – anything! Just *get it out!*"

Pete raised both his hands in desperation. "Please, calm yourselves! *Hold on*, everyone!" he cried at the top of his voice. At last the family fell into an uneasy silence.

"This really isn't a job for me," Pete continued. "There's a nice young chap who knows about this sort of thing – he's a biologist over at Rowan Park Wild Animal Sanctuary. Matthew Harding's his name. If I give him a ring, I'm sure he'll be able to help us."

"A *zoo?*" cried Zan, horrified. "Smoke will never go to a *zoo*. He'd rather *die* first. And *I'll* die before I let him!"

"It's not a zoo," Pete Barker assured him. "It's a sanctuary. A wonderful place, where – "

But his explanations were interrupted by another crash of furniture from inside Zan's room.

"Please use our telephone! I'm sure you'd like a nice, strong cup of tea too," Mrs. Makepeace offered, recovering enough to remember her social graces at last. She left hastily to make yet another pot of tea.

Her husband strode after her, still muttering darkly under his breath, "A *wolf?* A wolf in my house? Has the boy taken leave of his senses?"

Pete Barker had trouble tracking down Matthew Harding in the Rowan Park grounds, but at last he managed to find him. As Zan and Kibby sat listening on the stairs, they caught snatches of the most shocking conversation they had ever heard.

"Nine o'clock tomorrow morning, then.... Fine, Matthew, I'll be here.... You have access to the gun?... Yes, yes, it's the only answer. He's going crazy in there. Put him right out – much kinder, and safer!... For his own good.... All right, 'bye." He replaced the receiver. "Don't worry, it's all arranged," he told Mr. Makepeace, who had just come into the hall. "We'll be back for him tomorrow."

Zan glanced at Kibby. Her face was white. Obviously she too had heard what Pete Barker had said.

Zan felt sick and dizzy. "Kibby, they're going to *shoot* Smoke! Smoke trusted us. And now he's going to die and no one will listen to a single word we say!"

◆

That night, a sleepless Kibby got out of bed and went to the top of the stairs. She looked down into the sitting room. The sofa-bed where Zan was supposed to be sleeping lay empty, a blanket cast off into a heap on the floor nearby. There was a thin strip of light glowing from underneath his bedroom door across the hall. The room was supposed to be off limits until the morning, but Zan must have climbed in through the window.

Kibby crept down the stairs and tapped softly on the door. "Zan, it's me," she whispered. "Can I come in?"

As she entered, Smoke ran eagerly across the room to

greet her. Just for a second she hesitated, then she allowed him to lick her face all over, in his usual warm and sticky welcome. Kibby felt reassured. He was still the same lovable old Smoke. Even if he was a wolf now . . . .

Then Kibby noticed Zan's rucksack lying on the bed. Beside it lay a pile of T-shirts, two sweaters, a torch, and several other items. Something was wrong. "What are you doing?" she asked.

"Packing, Kibs. I'm leaving," her brother said. "I'm taking Smoke far away from here, so no one can ever find him again. They'll have to shoot *me* before I let them hurt a single hair on his body!"

"But where will you go?"

"To the country, I think." Zan did not really know where "the country" was, but it sounded like a fine place for a wolf to live. "No one'll ever find us there."

"Oh, Zan!" Kibby was wide-eyed and trembling. "Will you ever come back?"

"Maybe. Probably not."

"I don't s'pose I could come too?"

"No." Zan was hastily pushing the clothes into his rucksack. "Definitely not!"

He picked up his money box. It would not open, so he smashed it and quickly counted out his savings: twenty pounds towards a pair of the right make of trainers.

He selected three pound coins. "Here, Kibs," he said. "I want you to have these. You've been the best sister anyone could wish for. I won't be here for your birthday next week, so I'd like you to buy yourself the model showjump you wanted for Frosty."

"Oh, Zan, I can't," she protested. "You'll need – "

"Take them!" he ordered firmly, closing her chubby fingers around the coins. "Happy birthday, Kibs."

Kibby looked on helplessly as her brother pulled the window open and clicked his tongue to Smoke. He turned and gave her a brief, emotional hug, then climbed out the window. Smoke leapt out after him.

"Bye, Kibs," Zan whispered softly. "Take good care of Jenna for me." Then he was off, the wolf bounding along at his heels.

After they had disappeared into the darkness, Kibby could hear Zan's footsteps fading away along Tin Can Alley into the distance, leaving only the night sounds of the city suburbs behind.

CHAPTER EIGHT

Kibby quietly closed Zan's window and locked it. Trying her hardest not to cry, she picked up the computer keyboard from the floor and replaced it carefully on Zan's desk. Next she straightened out Smoke's mat under the bed, and finally she took her brother's cuddly seal pyjama-case from his pillow. Hugging it tightly for comfort, she switched off the light and left the room, fastening the door behind her.

She tiptoed silently up the stairs to her own room, placed the precious birthday money in her own small piggy-bank, then climbed back into bed, pulling the bed-clothes over her head.

◆

"Wake up, Kibby. Oh, *do* wake up!" For a wonderful moment she thought it was Zan. But as she sleepily opened her eyes, Kibby saw her mother standing beside the bed.

"Come *on*, Kibby! Mr. Barker and Matthew Harding

have arrived for Smoke. I can't find Zan anywhere. Do *you* know where he is?"

Mrs. Makepeace pulled back the bedclothes and began bundling Kibby into her dressing gown and slippers.

"Zan's gone, Mum. They both have," Kibby mumbled, still only half awake.

"What do you mean, gone?"

"He's run away, to save Smoke – he couldn't let them *kill* him!"

"*Kill* Smoke? Whatever are you talking about, dear?" Mrs. Makepeace marched her daughter out of the bedroom and down the stairs. There, her father and Pete Barker were waiting with a tall young man, who had a mop of curly brown hair and a beard. Presumably, he was Matthew Harding.

"Kibby says Zan's *gone*," Mrs. Makepeace announced.

Kibby felt four pairs of eyes staring at her. She burst into a torrent of angry tears. "He's run away, and it's *all your fault!*" she sobbed."Father Christmas brought him the *sweetest* puppy, after I wrote and asked him, and it's all been such fun! Zan's been so happy, and now you want to shoot Smoke, and everything's *ruined*, and, and" – she gasped for breath – "it's *just not fair!*"

Mr. and Mrs. Makepeace looked at each other, stunned by their daughter's outburst. They had never seen her so upset before.

But it was Matthew Harding who knelt down to speak to the sobbing child. "Hold on, now," he soothed, taking

hold of her hands. "No one's going to *shoot* Smoke. Whatever gave you *that* idea?"

"We heard Mr. Barker telling you to bring a *gun*,"
Kibby gulped. "'Put him out completely,' he said, 'for his
own good.'" Tears were pouring down her cheeks.

Now Matthew Harding understood what had happened.
"Oh, no, Kibby, you have it all wrong," he told her gently.
"We were talking about a dart gun – to tranquillize him.
Put him *temporarily* to sleep so that we could move him to
Rowan Park without upsetting him or hurting him in any
way. If Smoke's half as splendid as Mr. Barker says, he's a
very precious animal indeed. And he deserves a good life.
At the sanctuary he can live with dignity as a wild animal."

Kibby stamped her foot. "There was no need to tranquillize him!" she shouted angrily. "Zan's trained Smoke
to walk to heel – he takes him *everywhere* – sometimes he
even rides on the milk float!" Not caring how much of a
scene she was making, she screeched at the top of her
voice: "*Why wouldn't anybody LISTEN!*"

Matthew Harding stood up slowly, amazed.

Mrs. Makepeace looked wearily at her husband. "I'm
afraid we've handled this whole thing rather badly."

"With respect, I think you may have," Matthew
Harding said. "Although it's really not surprising."

"I'll call the police," said Mrs. Makepeace. "They'll find
them very quickly, I'm sure. After all, how far can one
young lad and a wolf go?"

"I think we should keep quiet about the wolf," Matthew

warned. "We don't want to start a national panic, or Zan and Smoke might get hurt."

"Yes, you're quite right," agreed Mrs. Makepeace. "We'll ask the police to fetch us as soon as Zan and his 'dog' are spotted. Then we can contact you straight away!" She hurried out of the room to telephone.

"Perhaps you'd better sit down," said Sam Makepeace, "and I'll go and put the kettle on. I think we could all do with a cup of tea." He went out to the kitchen.

Matthew Harding perched on the sofa beside Kibby. He had the friendliest grin the girl had ever seen, and she could not help but like him.

"Let me explain a little about wolves," the biologist began. "Long ago, when the whole planet – including most of Europe – was thickly forested, wolves were one of the most common animals; they roamed the woods in their thousands. But loss of habitat, plus the relentless persecution by man, eventually brought them to the brink of extinction in many parts of their former range."

Kibby had stopped sniffling by now, and she snuggled down comfortably beside her new friend as he continued his story.

"In most Western cultures, we've been taught to fear the wolf, from childhood onwards. All the folklore, and every fairy tale we've heard, tells us that the wolf is big and bad! Look at 'Little Red Riding Hood,' for one example."

Mrs. Makepeace re-entered the room and sat down to listen to Matthew.

"Yes, wolf packs *do* take larger prey like deer. They're ferocious predators; but they also live on smaller creatures such as rabbits and birds, or anything else they can find. There are hardly any instances on record of wolves attacking people, and most of those are probably tall stories or unfortunate accidents."

Mr. Makepeace, who had returned with the tea tray, paused in the doorway so as not to interrupt.

"Usually, it's quite the opposite," the biologist continued. "The wolf is *terrified* of humans – and with very good reason. Why, even today, the poor creatures are persecuted to death in many of the last few strongholds where they remain."

Matthew Harding paused and looked around. Everyone was listening intently, saddened by his tale.

"Now the most important thing to a wolf, old or young, is his *family*. They have one of the most sophisticated social systems known. They make loyal and loving parents, often stay together for life, and protect their offspring come hell or high water! The whole pack cooperates to ensure their survival." He turned to Mrs. Makepeace. "So you see," he told her, "Smoke wasn't *attacking* Kibby; he was just trying to protect *his* family, to save her from *you!* You were the danger threatening *her!* He'd have given his life to save her."

Mrs. Makepeace shook her head in dismay. "Oh dear, oh dear!"

"Of course, a young pup of Smoke's age is fairly adaptable," Matthew added, "but obviously wolves don't make good pets at all. By the time our chappie's a year old, he'll be nearly mature, and his wild instincts are bound to start showing through, despite his tame puphood. We must find Zan as soon as possible – who knows what might happen to a boy and a wolf out on the streets."

"Oh, Sam!" said June Makepeace tearfully to her husband, who was setting out the tea things. "All those *lies*. Just when we thought Zan was growing up and learning to be responsible at last!"

"Well, to be honest, I s'pose it was just one huge lie," Sam Makepeace replied, with a dry smile. He was feeling rather guilty.

Pete Barker gave him a sheepish glance and nodded in agreement. How he wished he'd made things clearer from the start!

"But I think Zan *must* have grown up," remarked Matthew Harding. "He's shown responsibility and dedication, really. To nurse a frozen wolf pup back from the brink of death and care for him all these months is quite an achievement – even for the experts, let alone in a bedroom, in secret."

"I helped too!" protested Kibby, finding her voice again at last. "We all learnt together!"

"Yes, I know you did, darling," Mrs. Makepeace smiled, "and I still don't know whether to praise you or scold you. I'm just so glad you didn't run away with them!" She gave Kibby a little hug and a kiss, but because

Matthew Harding was watching, Kibby grimaced and pulled away.

And, despite the gravity of the situation, the four adults burst out laughing.

◆

Two days later, journalist Tansy Briar called on the Makepeaces. Matthew Harding had told her the whole extraordinary tale over a candlelight supper for two the previous evening. Tansy was always on the lookout for a good story, and this could be her first real scoop, but she also genuinely wanted to help.

Kibby sat down on the settee beside the young woman and gazed at her in admiration. With her glossy chestnut hair and her brilliant red blouse and matching lipstick, to Kibby she looked like a film star.

"I won't mention anything about a wolf," Tansy assured the Makepeaces, "not until Zan and Smoke are safely back home again. But it's an amazing tale, and I do hope you'll let me write about it, once it has a happy ending."

"Yes, of course you can," Mrs. Makepeace agreed. "But where could that litter of pups have come from? Who'd be so incredibly cruel?"

Tansy shook her head. "Some people do awful things to animals. Matthew simply has no idea," she told them. "He'll do all he can to find out, though. The litter was probably from some shady dealer, or maybe an unwanted batch from an illegal exotic pet owner. The pups might have fetched a good price on the black market. So, really, it's something of a mystery.

"Anyway," she went on, getting up to leave, "I've made a few good contacts on the streets since I joined the *Satellite*. I'll go out today and see if I can find out if anyone has seen Zan and Smoke. Don't you worry – we'll have them back home safe and sound in no time!" She grinned at Kibby and added, "in plenty of time to go back to school, too!"

Kibby pulled a face. "Yech," she said. "Don't remind me!"

Tansy Briar sounded very confident, just as the police had done. But their hopes for Zan's speedy return soon faded away.

PART TWO

THE STREETS

CHAPTER NINE

The weather had finally broken, and large droplets of rain were splodging down onto the dusty pavement at Zan's feet as he walked. Around him, there was a general bustle of umbrellas going up and people quickening their footsteps to escape the summer downpour. Thunder rumbled across the skies. "Don't you worry – God must be moving his furniture!" Mrs. Makepeace would have said comfortingly. But for Zan, there was no cosy den in which to find solace. Just the harsh reality of the streets.

As the boy hurried through the crowds, carried along in the general momentum, Smoke kept close beside him, nose touching his master's jeans. The wolf was anxious, unsure of this sudden change of routine. Although he was well used to the suburban streets and the sight of strangers, the sheer numbers of people here in the heart of the city, along with the noise of the constant traffic whizzing by, was scaring him. He nosed Zan's hand and looked up for reassurance, but Zan, lost in thought, didn't notice.

The rain was coming down in sheets now, soaking Zan to the skin and pushing his hair down into his eyes. Around him, the pedestrians quickened their pace.

When it happened, Zan was hardly aware of it. He felt just a faint brushing motion as two youths passed by on either side of him and one of them lifted his rucksack from his shoulders.

"Hey!" he cried out, his voice drowned by a crash of thunder. "Stop!"

He ran a few paces forward and grabbed the rucksack, trying to tug it away, but the youths were too strong for him. His wallet fell to the ground and spilled open, sending four pound coins spinning onto the pavement.

Zan hesitated for a split second, and it was long enough. One of his attackers bent and grabbed the wallet, then disappeared after his companion into the crowd.

"Help! I've been robbed!" Zan called out. "Somebody stop them!"

But although one or two people stared curiously at him, no one did anything.

"Go on, Smoke, chase 'em, boy!" he urged.

But Smoke only nudged anxiously at his leg. For the first time, it occurred to Zan that Smoke was really nothing like a dog at all.

Zan started to collect the remaining coins. One of them

had rolled into the gutter, and an old lady had spotted it. She bent down, picking it carefully out of the torrents of storm water, and shook it dry. Zan was on the point of thanking her when she put it into her own pocket and hobbled off along the road with only a hasty glance behind her.

Stunned, Zan stood for a moment or two as life carried on around him. Eventually his instinct for survival took over. He was soaked and shivering. He had to find shelter from the rain.

Spotting the entrance to a tiny church hall nearby, he ran quickly up the flagstone steps and into the porch. There he sat, trembling, with Smoke at his feet, as the rain cascaded onto the roof above him.

The downpour stopped as suddenly as it had begun. Within seconds a warm, hazy sun was shining down onto the steamy wet streets, and people were beginning to emerge from the shop doorways, hurrying and scurrying about like ants pouring out of a broken nest, streaming down the pavements, frantically resuming their business.

Zan moved out into the sun too, and sat down on the top step to dry off. He patted the adjacent flagstone, which was beginning to steam in the warmth.

"Here, Smoke," he encouraged, and obligingly the wolf settled down beside him, chin on paws. Like his master, he was confused and concerned.

As they sat there, gradually the impact of everything that had happened began to sink in. Overwhelmed, Zan buried his face in his hands, as if to shut out the whole world.

"You all right, mate?" A voice in his ear made him jump. He turned to see a boy, somewhat smaller and maybe a year or two younger than himself, seated on his right. The boy was thin and incredibly scruffy, with grimy jeans and long sandy-coloured hair which was crying out for a cut. But to Zan his friendly smile was pure gold.

"I've just been mugged!" Zan said. "They took everything I had, except for three pound coins."

"What did they look like?"

Zan told him, and the boy nodded in recognition. "That'd be Mickey and Bugs."

"You *know* them?"

"Well, they're not my friends, but I know *of* them. I know everyone on the streets," replied the boy. "If you like, I can get some of your stuff back later on. I know just where they'll dump anything they don't want. I can't stand waste!" He gave Zan a wink.

Zan stared in amazement at his new friend, who went on brightly, "Must've thought you were a tourist – they usually choose tourists." Then he added more sympathetically, "Bad luck, mate!"

"*Only* tourists? Jolly welcoming! What total rats!" Zan exclaimed angrily.

This outburst made his companion smile again. Then a puzzled look crossed the boy's face. "Isn't the three pounds enough for your bus fare home, mate?"

"I have no home," Zan said quietly. "I've run away. I'm going to the country." Finally speaking the words aloud made him sound far braver than he really felt.

Now it was his companion's turn to look amazed. "No kidding? Did your Dad thump *you* too? Awful, isn't it?" He sighed. "I've been out here for nearly two years now. Oh, by the way, I'm Five.' He paused, waiting for Zan to comment, and when Zan did not, he went on, "Frederick Ive. Seriously – gross, isn't it? *F. Ive* – see?"

Zan saw. "Alexander James Makepeace," he returned. "Zan for short. And this is my wo– er, my dog – Smoke."

"Nice," murmured Five politely, scratching Smoke's head. It was obvious that he wasn't one of the world's greatest dog lovers.

Smoke tapped his tail tip lightly on the pavement in response.

"D'you live near here?" Zan asked.

"Not very far away. With Granpop, under the Archway. He's not my real grandfather, of course, but he looked out for me when I first came to the city. He's not so well nowadays, so we take care of him instead. He was a real soldier, you know. He can tell you all about the war – he was *there!*" Five finished proudly.

"How many more of you live around here?"

"Well, Tebs and Jake share our patch, but there are plenty of others nearby. You'd like Beckie and Tiza – they're sisters, and they're really nice. Not like girls at all! Tiza has a dog too – a greyhound named Ziggy. Sometimes Beckie cooks us all a huge pot of veggie stew. It's the best!" Five was well into his stride by now. "I'll take you to meet them if you want...." The boy paused to draw breath, then added, "I'd forget about the country if I were you, mate. The country's for cows and sheep. Too green! What would you eat – grass? Are you hungry now?"

"*Starving!*" replied Zan with feeling.

Five laughed heartily. Zan certainly didn't look as though he were starving! In fact, by street standards – or by anyone else's – his companion looked more than a little overweight.

Zan frowned, and at once Five appeared suitably contrite.

"Your three pounds would buy us both beans on toast at the Golden Egg," he suggested hopefully. Five was never short on cheek!

Food! It sounded wonderful to Zan, and he certainly wasn't going to bear any grudges at this point.

"All right, let's blow the lot, then!" he cried recklessly, jumping to his feet.

"Good for you, mate! Five said. "Hey, I knew today would turn out to be different! That's half the fun of the streets. You never know what'll happen next!"

With Smoke bounding at their heels, glad to be on the move again, the two boys set off along the pavement towards the railway. Zan, too, felt good to be heading somewhere at last.

The violent storm had washed and blow-dried the city

streets. Now they stretched away, luxuriously clean and sparkling with mirrored puddles of rainwater which reflected the cloudless blue of the sky. For now, even the air itself smelt fresh and sweet. It was a pleasure to breathe – and great to be alive!

"Luckily, my dog's already eaten," Zan informed Five as they marched briskly along in step. "He found a whole portion of fish and chips beside a litter bin, near the dolphin fountain."

"A *whole portion?* And you let him have it?" Five spun round, aghast.

"It was lying on the pavement. Who knows where it had been?" Zan protested. "And there were flies around it too!"

"You'll soon learn, my boy," Five assured him.

CHAPTER TEN

 Zan followed Five through the entrance to the Archway, into the gloomy atmosphere beyond. The air inside felt cool, but it smelt stale and sooty.

"Home sweet home!" Five sang out, only half-joking as he turned to Zan with a grin. "Cool in summer, warm in winter, and when it rains – running water too. Perfect. Who could ask for more? Come on, mate!" He quickened his step, leading his new friend on.

Soon the tunnel opened out into a more spacious area, lit only from above by some filthy, half-broken skylights. At once Zan could see several camps, distinguishable by their piles of cardboard boxes and the odd tatty mattress lying on the ground.

As Zan's sight adjusted to the gloom, he could make out people. Some were huddled in small groups, some sitting alone with empty faces.

Five led him to a nearby cluster of boxes, perched

untidily around a central brazier. "The best patch!" he told Zan proudly. "The Mayfair of the Archway! This is where I live. And here's Granpop."

An old man was seated on a broken orange box near the brazier. He had long white hair and a white beard which gave him the appearance of Old Father Time himself. His crinkled face was as weathered as a walnut, but his blue eyes twinkled as he greeted Zan with an almost toothless smile.

"Ah, there you are, Five my boy. I was wondering where you'd been all day!"

"Granpop, this is Zan," said Five.

"Hello, son." Granpop's voice was croaky with age. He held out both hands, knobbly and arthritic, and shook Zan's warmly.

Even though the late summer's evening was warm, the old man wore an ancient overcoat which had definitely seen better days.

"Zan's run away from home. They wanted to shoot Smoke, his dog here," Five explained. "Mickey and Bugs mugged him, but I'm going to get back his things. Can he stay with us, please, Granpop?"

"Five, I've warned you before, stay away from those two thugs. They're bad news!" A deep, well-spoken voice rang out behind them. "One day you'll really be hurt."

Zan turned to see a tall, brown-haired young man in his early twenties standing behind them.

"Yes, Mum!" said Five cheekily, and was rewarded with a playful rap on his head.

"Don't you 'Yes Mum' me, Shrimp – you know perfect-ly well I'm right!"

Five ducked away laughing. "This is Tebs," he told Zan. "He's worse than my mother. Nag, nag, nag – keeps us all tied to his apron strings!" Their good-natured banter made Zan feel much more comfortable, as though at last he was really among friends again.

Then he noticed that Tebs was not alone. Standing just behind him was a shorter chap with jet-black hair and a pallid complexion. Zan drew a sharp breath as he recognized the boy he had surprised in his room at home.

"You!"

"You know Jake?" asked Tebs.

"Well, we met once, briefly," Zan explained quickly.

As Jake skirted warily around Smoke, he muttered, "How the mighty have fallen!"

"Young Zan will be staying with us for a while, boys," Granpop told them firmly. "I hope you'll look out for him too. He's one of us now."

Neither Tebs nor Jake looked very enthusiastic at this prospect, but then Tebs offered a little more kindly, "You'll need a good strong cardboard box before the weather turns. The warehouse stocks up tomorrow morning, so there'll be plenty in the back yard. Spin driers are the best, but we'll have to go early, or–"

"Or all the best boxes will be taken!" Zan joked, but no one else laughed. There was an awkward pause.

"The girls'll be back soon," said Five, tactfully changing

the subject. "You'll like them a lot."

And indeed, within a few minutes, Beckie and Tiza, two pretty girls of about sixteen and fourteen, had appeared. Their arms were filled with bags containing a variety of fresh, if rather battered-looking, vegetables.

"We help in the market on Fridays," Beckie explained after the introductions were complete. "There are always enough leftovers to make a good hot veggie stew for all of us. Whose turn is it to cook today?"

"Mine," admitted Tebs unwillingly, and everyone groaned.

"It's not that Tebs minds cooking," Tiza explained to Zan, "it's just that we mind eating it!"

"He's definitely the worst of the lot!" Granpop smiled without a trace of rancour. "Beckie's sure he sneaks Five's old socks in, just to make it taste really dreadful. That way he won't be asked to cook again!"

"I *don't!*" cried Tebs, pretending to be deeply hurt. "It'll be delicious tonight, you wait and see! The best yet!"

"*Sock au vin*, more likely!"

"Well, Zan and I don't need any," said Five, looking relieved. "We've already eaten."

"But that was *lunch!*" protested Zan. He could not understand why everyone seemed so amused at his remark.

Smoke, who had been sitting quietly between Zan and Granpop, shuffled forward. Tiza gave a cry of surprise and leant over to pet him.

"So you're the cause of all the trouble, eh?" She cradled his face in her hands and kissed the top of his head. "Oh, Zan, he's *gorgeous!* Those yellow eyes and the silver coat make him look almost wolf-like."

"Almost," Zan agreed uncomfortably.

"I like the mask," remarked Tebs. "He looks like the Lone Ranger."

"The Lone *who?*"

"Before your time, my son!"

Smoke licked Tiza's face. The youngster was the nearest thing to Kibby he'd found yet, and already he missed the little girl so much.

"Come on then, wolfy-chops. You must meet Ziggy – I'll go and fetch her!" Tiza said, jumping to her feet. "A friend's been looking after her today – we thought the market would be far too hot."

"But instead we got drenched!" smiled Beckie.

"Me too!" said Zan.

"Still, it'll save washing tonight!" Five chipped in, and he wasn't joking.

"Since when did you ever wash?" Tebs asked him with a grin.

"Christmas!"

"The one before last?"

"No, when he was *baptised!*"

With supper over they all sat lazily around the fire, chatting away late into the warm August night and listening to Tebs play the blues on his mouth organ.

◆

That first night, Zan hardly slept a wink, although Five had kindly shared his mattress. While the others snored around him, he had tossed and turned as his exhausted body began to ache, unaccustomed to the hard ground. Without a blanket the night hours were surprisingly cold.

The boy thought longingly of his soft, comfortable bed at home. He was also hungry again, but of course there would be no breakfast. He could not go into the larder and help himself to three Zan-sized bowls of Oatie Crunch as usual. With a deep sigh, he closed his eyes again, hoping someone else would wake up soon. Suddenly, he had never felt so alone.

Tebs was as good as his word. At eight-thirty, they helped Granpop along to the market, for his arthritis was very bad despite the summer warmth. They left him sitting with an old friend called The Duke to await the morning food round of the Helping Hands organisation.

"Hot coffee and bacon butties usually," Tebs remarked to Zan, as they made their way with a reluctant Jake along the streets towards the warehouse. It sounded wonderful to Zan, but as no one else seemed bothered about breakfast, he tried hard to ignore his hunger pangs.

Beckie and Tiza had fed Smoke that morning. Proper dog food, bought for Ziggy with the little money Beckie earned hairdressing. She had started her training at home, before she and Tiza had been forced to leave.

"Don't worry," Tiza had assured Zan, "we'll make sure he doesn't go hungry, until you sort yourself out."

"Typical!" Jake had sneered. "Those wretched dogs eat better than we do!" It was true. Every dog Zan saw on the streets was in peak condition, toned with muscle and glossy-coated. To some people, their pets were the only friends in the world, and when there was only a little food, the animals ate first.

The smell of dog food had always made Zan feel a little sick. But soon its rich, meaty odour was as tempting as a prime steak and kidney pie.

He realized very early on, having left home blindly on that fateful night, that his ideas of keeping himself and Smoke fed and healthy while on the run had been way off the mark. 'Cloud cuckoo land,' his mother would have said. He had been extremely fortunate to meet up with such good friends.

◆

The new washing machine box provided Zan with a place of his own. There was plenty of room inside for him and Smoke. Tipped on its side, with the flaps pulled together, the thick cardboard box shut out the noise and the draughts, and provided a welcome sanctuary from the world outside, which was frequently none too pleasant, even in the Archway.

In the nights that followed, as he lay on an old cot mattress, with a torn but clean blanket which Beckie had obtained from the Rescue Centre, Zan's stiff, aching muscles gradually grew accustomed to his new bed. Sleep came at last. Smoke acted as both a hot water bottle and a pillow. Despite Jake's jibes about fleas (and who was he to talk!) Zan always allowed the wolf to sleep in his box. He needed to feel the strong comforting presence beside him as the night-timers roamed around outside, coming so close sometimes that one could even hear them breathing. The clinking of bottles and the cursing of the winos were far removed from Kibby's innocent pleas for a bedtime story at home.

"You and your privacy," Tebs frequently teased him. "One day I expect you'll be putting a padlock on that box or wiring it up with a burglar alarm!" And how often Zan wished that he could!

CHAPTER ELEVEN

Tebs had enjoyed an excellent morning's busking, playing his harmonica for the last of the summer tourists who were still milling about the city. He had bought a pile of ham sandwiches and brought them back to the Archway to share with anyone else who was at home.

Zan and Granpop had been deep in conversation all morning about war-time aircraft. Spitfires and Lancasters were the old man's favourites. When Tebs arrived, Granpop called Tiza over too, to enjoy a share in the feast.

At last, Zan found the right moment to question the young girl about her home. As he stroked Ziggy's soft brindled coat, he asked, "Did you leave the North because of your dog too?"

"Heavens, no!" exclaimed Tiza, selecting another sandwich. "We found Ziggy wandering along the railway line about a year ago. You can see from the white hairs on her muzzle that she's quite old – too old to be any more use as a racing greyhound. Obviously she was dumped, poor little soul. But *we* take good care of you now, don't we, sweetheart?" She hugged the dog tightly, and Ziggy's limp tail began to wag. Smoke's ears pricked up with interest too, as Zan offered him a crust of bread.

"So why did you leave?" he persevered.

Tiza looked away uneasily. There was a pause. "It was because of our new stepfather," she said at last. "He was really vile to us, but Mum would never believe it. She called us both troublemakers – so we left. We just couldn't stand him any longer. She chose him over us, her own children. Beckie said she'd never forgive her."

"Won't your Mum be *worried*, though?"

"Won't yours?"

Now it was Zan's turn to look uncomfortable. It was something he hadn't thought about much. "I suppose she might be. Probably not."

He had felt so angry with his parents, and so betrayed by them, that he tried hard not to consider their feelings. And he missed Kibby so badly, he could hardly bear to think about her at all.

"What's the time?" asked Granpop, quickly moving the conversation on to a lighter topic. He could see the pain in the boy's eyes.

"Nearly three o'clock," Zan replied, and Granpop turned to Tebs.

"I'm a little concerned about young Five," he said. "He

was only going off for an hour this morning, and he's still not back."

"Would you like me to go and look for him?" suggested Tebs. "He may have got into some trouble with Mickey and Bugs. You know Five. The little blighter thinks he's invincible! I'd rather take Jake, but" – he glanced over at Zan – "*you'll* have to do. I suppose you'd better bring that furry mutt of yours along too, even though he couldn't say boo to a mouse!"

"It's a goose," Zan pointed out. "Boo to a *goose*."

"Ever seen any geese round here, kid?"

◆

When they reached the noisy amusement arcade, Tebs stopped.

"Better wait outside," he told Zan. "I'll just have a scout round inside and see if I can spot Five." He vanished into the crowd.

Within seconds Zan found a scruffy teenage boy and girl beside him. They were very friendly, introducing themselves as Steve and Annie and offering him multi-coloured sweets. And they made a huge fuss over Smoke. When Annie mentioned her birthday party, Zan started to accept politely, then suddenly he found himself being lifted right off the ground by the scruff of his neck. Steve and Annie ran off.

"You need to learn the difference," Tebs roared at him, "between the *good* ones and the *bad* ones! If you're going to survive out here, you need to start using your *brains!*"

"Ow!" Zan protested. "Let go, you're hurting me!" Now he was scared. "I didn't know they were doing anything wrong!"

"Granpop's golden rule," Tebs continued. "Drugs are for mugs. Now say it! Go on!"

"Drugs are for mugs!" Zan spluttered.

Tebs set him down on the pavement. "You ever break that rule, and you're out, finished. Understand? Not just with *us*, but with *life!*"

"Yes," Zan replied meekly. He understood. And he never forgot it.

◆

"Five might have come here looking for your stolen belongings," Tebs said as he led Zan down a litter-strewn street. He stopped outside one house in a derelict row at the far end. The houses were obviously due for demolition, with their windows boarded and their rooftops scarred with vast holes as though they had been bombed. The front walls were covered with colourful graffiti, probably the handiwork of the squatters inside. The whole area was run-down, a truly dismal and depressing place. It made the Archway look positively posh.

Tebs rapped sharply on the faded door. After a while, it was opened by one of the youths who had mugged Zan. He was wearing a torn leather jacket with "Bugs" scrawled on the pocket. He didn't recognise Zan. To him the boy was just another faceless victim, and Zan quickly felt the anger rising inside him. But he left the talking to Tebs.

"We're looking for Five. We don't want any trouble."

"Five what?" asked Bugs, and began to laugh. The other mugger, presumably Mickey, appeared at the door behind him.

Tebs carried on. "We know he's here – we're not leaving without him."

"Are you and the Boy Wonder here going to beat us up, then?" Bugs sneered.

Mickey said, "He's working for us now. He won't be going anywhere with you again. Ever."

Zan's temper snapped. "He would *never* work for you two – *never!*" he cried out.

In the brief pause afterwards, Smoke pricked up his ears and gave a short bark. He had heard something – a faint cry for help?

"Look at Smoke! He knows Five is in there," Tebs said, and he and Zan took a step forward. But Mickey and Bugs blocked the doorway. It looked as though things might become very unpleasant indeed.

But Smoke was also learning to be street-wise. Now *he* could tell the difference between good folk and bad folk. He could sense Zan's fear, and it made him angry. The wolf could also remember the amazing effect he had had on Mr. and Mrs. Makepeace during that last evening in Sunfield. So he raised his hackles, bared his gleaming white fangs, and growled as menacingly as he could. He looked awesome!

Mickey and Bugs leapt away from the door, trying to escape the wolf's vicious-looking jaws.

"You'd better keep still," Zan told them smugly, "or my dog will tear you into bite-sized pieces!"

"Call 'im off," croaked Bugs in terror.

Zan's confidence was soaring. "Don't make him angry – he's trained to protect me!"

Tebs was already down the corridor, opening up each door in turn, searching for Five.

"Guard them, boy!" Zan instructed Smoke, and went quickly in pursuit of his friend.

Zan and Tebs came at last to a locked door. From behind it, they could hear Five's muffled squeaks.

"Hey, I'm in here! Get me out!"

"Five, stand back! We'll have to break down the door!" Tebs shouted. "It should be easy enough – it's almost rotten anyway." Together he and Zan ran at it, shoulders braced for the impact.

The rusty old hinges gave way, sending the entire door crashing inwards onto the floor. Swirling clouds of dust rose into the rays of afternoon sunshine which streamed in through a tiny window.

Five was huddled in a corner. "Am I glad to see you, mate!" he announced fervently. "You too, Zanno!" A large bruise was beginning to form on his left cheek.

"You look like Chi-Chi the panda!" Tebs told him affectionately. "Come on, Shrimp, let's get you out of here!"

"Thanks, Mum. I owe you one."

"Watch it, kid, or I'll thump you!"

When they were a safe distance down the road, Zan called to Smoke, and the wolf came bounding after them, tail wagging, tongue lolling, and a big wolfy grin spread across his muzzle. If a wolf can look smug, Smoke did. He knew he had done well.

Five began to make an enormous fuss of him. Suddenly he liked dogs a great deal more than before. "Smoke the Wonder Dog. What a brave old fellow you are!"

Jake came hurrying round the corner. He looked taken aback to see them all. "Granpop sent me to help," he told them, "but obviously you don't need me."

"Zan and Smoke were wonderful!" crowed Five. "Oh, Jake, you should have seen them!"

Jake gave him a rather tepid smile. "Glad you're safe, anyway. You *are* an idiot, Five!"

"Oh," cried Five, fishing about in his pocket. "I found something for you, Zan." With a flourish, he produced Zan's wallet. "But they must have got rid of your rucksack and your clothes already."

"Oh, thank you!" Zan was delighted to have part of his property back again, even though he didn't have a penny to put in it.

"And there's more," Five went on. He waved a small wad of bank notes in front of Tebs's nose.

"Where on earth did you find those?" Jake exclaimed.

"I 'borrowed' them from Mickey! Finders keepers, I say. Not such an idiot now, am I, Jakey?"

Tebs gave a sharp burst of laughter. "Five, you really are the limit! They'll have your guts for garters next time!"

"There won't be a next time," Five assured him. "They'd have to catch me first, and I won't be *that* stupid again!" He gave a grin. "And talking of guts, does anyone fancy a monster fry-up at the Golden Egg?"

◆

As the little group wandered home along the riverbank, the scene was bathed in the rosy pink glow of the setting sun. Spirits were high. They always were, when one felt pleasantly full – a rarity to those who lived on the streets.

The enormous plane trees which overhung the water were showing the first hints of autumn's gilding, and a shallow layer of crispy brown leaves crunched deliciously on the pathway underfoot. It was a glorious evening.

Five picked up a small stick and threw it on ahead for Smoke, who ignored it.

"See that, Zan?" Five called out in amazement. "Your dog can't even fetch sticks. Doesn't he know how to *play?*"

Zan didn't answer. In all honesty, he felt that teaching an animal useless tricks was rather demeaning. But he wasn't going to start splitting hairs now with someone who had just treated him to double sausage, egg, beans, tomatoes, and chips.

"I'll teach him," declared Five. He began hurling more

sticks high into the air. "Here, Smokey – fetch, boy. Oh, go on, you daft dog!"

Smoke turned his attention to some geese on the river-bank nearby. But Five wasn't giving up that easily. Getting down onto his hands and knees, he fetched the stick himself.

"Look, like this, *see!*"

Zan, Tebs, and Jake laughed so hard at Five's antics that they had to sit down on the grass to recover.

Eventually Smoke, who appeared thoroughly bored with the whole affair, trotted slowly over to a large fallen branch. Picking it up carefully in his strong jaws, he carried it solemnly over and presented it to Five.

"I've *done* it!" the boy shouted, jumping up and down in triumph. "I've trained him, now he's a *normal* dog!"

As Zan sat and laughed with the others, a rare sweet feeling of peace and relief settled over him. He was warm and well-fed, and he had made some wonderful friends. His new life on the city streets was going to be just fine after all.

CHAPTER TWELVE

 In October, the weather turned noticeably colder almost overnight, and brought with it a new and desperate routine. With the warmth of the summer gone, life became literally a question of staying alive.

Cold and hunger were the worst enemies of those on the streets. Zan and his friends, with their cardboard boxes clustered around the fire in the Archway, were among the more fortunate ones. At least they didn't have to sleep in the shop doorways, where the icy draughts chilled even the toughest of souls right through to the marrow.

Everyone grew to depend more and more on the Helping Hands soup run and, whenever they could reach it, the nearest soup kitchen too. Once a day, dozens of cold and weary folk gathered there in long queues, faces blank with despair, as they waited silently for a life-saving hand-out.

"This just can't go on – I have to find work!" Zan told

Smoke over and over again, as each new dawn broke across the city. But it was easier said than done. Without a home address, there could be no job. And without a job, no home. It was the same frustrating old problem, taking him round and round in circles, as day after day the boy found himself turned away.

"I'm sorry, lad, can't help – no vacancies." Even when Zan felt sure that there were.

"One final newsagent to try today!" Zan said to Smoke one dreary morning. "This time maybe we'll be lucky." He huddled closer to the fire for a hasty warm-up before braving the bitter cold outside.

That morning, the boy's spirits were particularly low. Everyone had caught colds recently, and at night the Archway echoed with the endless sound of coughing. Resistance to illness was very low among the homeless, and any infections spread quickly.

Granpop's cold had been much worse than the others' because of his age. He had not been able to fight it off, and his frailty was becoming quite a worry.

Zan was no longer overweight. He looked thin and pale, and his hair and clothing were as shabby as the next person's. He didn't even possess a winter coat to protect him from the biting north wind.

Smoke was faring rather better. The cold weather didn't seem to bother him at all. He had grown his own thick woolly winter undercoat, and he was finding enough food to survive, one way or another. For company, he had Zan and his new family of Five, Tiza, and Ziggy. What more could a wolf need?

◆

"I'm sorry, lad, there are no vacancies," the newsagent repeated impatiently, keen for him to leave.

"Please, couldn't I do *something – anything?* I'm good at delivering papers. I'm cheap, and very reliable." Zan had become used to begging.

"There's nothing here." The man took two bags of potato crisps off the shelf and tossed them in Zan's direction. "Here – take these. Now scram, kid. You're keeping my regulars away!"

Outside in the street a young woman wearing a smart white mackintosh stood talking to a group of people. She showed them a photograph, but one by one they shook their heads and began to drift off.

Tossing back her chestnut hair, the woman sighed. It had been a frustrating morning.

"Thanks anyway," she said and began to walk slowly away.

Zan came out of the newsagent's, head bent as he tried to open a crisp packet with his teeth. He almost bumped straight into her. "Oops, sorry!"

"That's all right," said the woman. And, as Tansy Briar headed off down the street, Smoke, seeing Zan, came out from behind the litter bin where he had been sitting quietly, waiting for his master.

◆

After wandering dispiritedly for an hour or more, Zan found himself at the rear of the High Street, in the back yard of the little Italian restaurant known as Alassi's. Set conveniently on a busy street corner, it was a popular eating place for local business people. The boy had often stopped to stare through the steamy front windows, enviously watching the diners as they sat chatting cosily around their tables. If he lingered too long, someone would wave a fist at him and mouth "Clear off!" as if he were no more than a stray dog. Now the appetizing smells which wafted across the yard from the kitchen extractor fan were almost too much to bear.

Smoke stood up on his hind legs and buried his nose deep in one of the dustbins. Often there was a stale piece of meat or some cold but edible pasta to be found in there. Stretching down further to reach a particularly tasty morsel, he rocked the dustbin off balance and pulled it right over. It crashed onto the cobblestones, spilling its contents in all directions. The back door of the restaurant opened, and Zan ducked down behind another bin.

A middle-aged man came out. The first thing which struck Zan was his enormous girth – he was completely round. His cheerful, rosy face was like a huge, pink beach ball. His head was almost bald, except for a fringe of black hair hanging along his collar at the back. A black and white apron was tied loosely around his waist. He looked like one of those dolls which bounce back upright when you push them over.

Smoke cowered. He was expecting a tirade of abuse, but instead the man bent down to pat him, speaking with an Italian accent. "What a beautiful boy you are! But what a mess you make, eh? Are you looking for food, *bambino mio?*"

Zan slipped cautiously into view. "I'm really sorry, sir," he said. "He's my dog. I'll clear it all up for you, I promise."

The man looked up with a friendly smile. "Who are you?" he asked, staring at the scruffy waif standing before him.

"I'm Zan Makepeace, sir, and this is Smoke." Zan was making sure of his manners.

"Well, hello, Zan Makepeace. And where do *you* come from, eh? I haven't seen you here before."

"I'm staying in the Archway, with Granpop and some other friends."

"Grandapop? I haven't seen him for a long time now. How is the old fella?"

"Not very well, I'm afraid – he has arthritis, and a bad chest with the cold weather."

"You tell him Carlo Alassi will be along one day soon to see him." Then he asked Zan, "Are you hungry too?"

"*Starving*, sir!"

"I tell you what I do. You clean my yard, and I go find you something to eat. You and Smokey here. There's plenty leftovers today." And before Zan could reply, the man had turned and disappeared inside. He reappeared within seconds carrying a large broom.

Zan swept the yard carefully, then tapped anxiously on the door. He had learnt not to take anything for granted on the streets. But Mr. Alassi welcomed him like an old friend, ushering him into the hot steamy kitchen, where the smell of food brought him close to fainting with anticipation.

On the table sat the most *enormous* dish of spaghetti and meatballs he had ever seen. And there was a huge bowl of it on the floor for Smoke.

As fast as the boy ate, the kindly Italian spooned more onto the plate, until at last Zan said, "Oh, Mr. Alassi, I couldn't eat another thing. Honestly, I'm just not *used* to it!" He felt sure if he swallowed one more mouthful, spaghetti would start wriggling out of his ears! And he could see Smoke's stomach bulging underneath his ribcage.

But Mr. Alassi was not satisfied. "You are too thin. We have to feed you up!" he grinned. Then he asked, "Do you want to work, Zan? You make such a good job of my yard. Such a strong boy!"

"Oh, yes please, sir," Zan replied eagerly. "I can be as strong as an ox."

Mr. Alassi thought for a moment. "I tell you what I do," he said, beaming even more widely. "You can come and work for me three afternoon a week. Is only cleaning and washing dishes. But it must be good, or I have the Health Authority on my back, now that my Luisa's gone! I pay you, and you and Smokey here eat as much as you like when you finish."

Zan could hardly believe his luck. "Oh, thank you – *grazie*, Signor Alassi!" he cried, remembering his first Italian lessons from school. He shook the man's podgy hand over and over. Money, and three guaranteed meals a week! What *unbelievable* good fortune at last!

Zan's feet hardly seemed to touch the pavement as he strode homeward, whistling a cheerful tune, with Smoke jogging contentedly at his heels. His spirits were high, and his stomach was full. All was right with the world!

Mr. Alassi had also insisted on paying Zan for sweeping his yard. So, for the first time since leaving home, Zan had money in his wallet. He felt ten feet tall!

Making his way back towards the Archway, he found himself outside the little church hall where he had sheltered from the storm on his first day in the city. The doors were wide open. On the step was a notice board which announced:

JUMBLE SALE – TODAY!
Doors open 2.30 : Teas

A man sweeping in the doorway saw Zan and called, "We're just closing, son. Come in now if you want a quick look round. There's still plenty left to buy."

"Thank you, sir. May I bring in my dog?"

"Of course you can, son, but hurry up now."

Tables were spread round the outer edges of the hall, some still laden with items for sale. As soon as he saw the low prices, Zan's heart began to pound with excitement. He could buy presents! Now he could afford to say thank you to his new friends for everything they had done for him.

But his first purchase was for himself. A thick, navy blue duffle coat – probably a ladies', but he didn't care. It was warm and fitted perfectly, and it cost him only fifty pence. Never before had the fashion bullies at school seemed quite so pathetic.

He selected a jersey each for Tebs and Jake, and two pairs of woolly socks for Five, who was always complaining about cold feet. He added a warm scarf for Tiza, and for Beckie he bought a real luxury, because he had missed her birthday: a glorious little crystal necklace. It glittered every colour of the rainbow under the artificial lights, and he was sure she'd love it! Among the battered paperbacks on the bookstall, he found a wonderful old volume called *Wings of the War*, packed with pictures of every aircraft imaginable, for Granpop.

Finally, a cluster of cutlery caught his eye. Odd knives, forks, and spoons, all tied loosely together with a piece of tatty string. Eagerly, he spent his last few pence on those.

"Fancy a cuppa, dearie?" an elderly woman asked him with a bright smile. "The pot's still warm."

"Yes please!" Zan thought he had died and gone to

heaven. He was presented with a steaming mug of tea and two large jam doughnuts. For weeks he had been so hungry he feared he might not survive, and now people were virtually *throwing* food at him! When no one was looking, the boy tucked the doughnuts into his pocket to take home for the food pool. Five and Jake would no doubt make short work of them later.

"I've something else you might like, dearie," the woman remarked, returning to his side.

"I'm afraid I've got no money left!"

"It's all right, dear, we've had a good day, and the sale's for the homeless, you know." She held out a red leather collar. "I thought your dog might look much smarter in this rather than with that old piece of rope round his neck. You take it, dear, my treat."

The tip of Smoke's tail was waving. He could sense kindness. He nudged Zan's hand with his nose in encouragement.

"Thank you very much," Zan said. "It's brilliant."

Altogether it had been an extraordinary day. But hadn't Five always said that street life could be full of surprises?

◆

By the time Zan reached the Archway everyone else was already home.

"My word, here comes Father Christmas, and so *early* this year!" quipped Tebs as Zan approached, staggering under the weight of his purchases.

"I've found a job and brought you all presents!" he announced, then, accidentally tripping over Ziggy, he landed in a tangled heap on the ground at their feet. Barking with delight, Smoke and Ziggy dived on top of him, and so did Five. It was not quite the entrance Zan had planned.

"Get off, you idiots! Ow, that's my leg!"

But Granpop's pale eyes misted with memories as soon as he saw his book.

"Thank you, son," he whispered, his weathered old hands trembling in anticipation, as he turned the illustrated pages. Five was so thrilled with his new socks that he threw the old ones straight onto the fire. This was a terrible idea, as everyone else soon discovered.

"Phwoar!"

"Toasted cheese!"

"Pull 'em off, Five, before we all *suffocate!*"

Beckie put on her necklace, her eyes sparkling as brightly as the crystals themselves, and danced a little polka with Zan round the brazier.

"Wonderful, *wonderful!*" she sang. "I feel like the Queen of Sheba!"

Tiza, spotting the cutlery, cried out in amusement, "Oh Zan! Real spoons and *forks!* Wherever did you find them? Now we can dine in style!"

"Good grief," jeered Jake. "Soon we'll be using napkins, and there'll be a vase of flowers on the table as well. Do we have to *dress* for dinner?"

Tebs began to laugh. "And high time too! Let's teach Five some manners. I say, Zan, any chance of some Royal Doulton china?"

"Take no notice of them," said Tiza hastily. "They're only jealous."

And she was right. How Jake wished *he'd* bought the presents and made Beckie's eyes shine like the morning sun on the canal. "Creep," the lad grumbled ungraciously. "You toady round old Lassie for a couple of minutes, and land yourself a cushy job. Talk about the luck of the devil!"

"Shut up, Jake," said Beckie. "Don't be so mean."

Zan looked concerned. "I'm sure Mr. Alassi could find you some work too, if you'd like it," he offered. "I'll ask him on Friday."

"I'm not cleaning dirty floors for anyone, and I certainly don't need your charity!" returned Jake, and tossed his new jersey onto the brazier. "*That's* what I think of your present!"

Hackles rising, Smoke delivered a warning growl from deep within his throat.

"And I never did trust that flea-bitten mongrel of yours. Those awful yellow eyes are too shifty by half!" Jake stormed away into the night. Smoke followed him a few yards down the tunnel, but padded obediently back when Tiza called his name.

Zan was crestfallen. Biting his lip, he stared glumly down at his feet, close to tears.

"Don't mind him," Beckie soothed, quickly rescuing

the jersey from the flames. "It's only a bit singed. Your presents are excellent, Zan. You really have made a difference."

And somehow, her words made the whole thing worthwhile after all.

"I'll have the jersey," piped up Five, "if nobody else wants it."

Tiza settled down comfortably beside Granpop. She wound the tail end of her scarf around his neck and gave him a hug.

"How are you feeling now, Granpop?" she asked the old man. "Are you strong enough to tell us all about your part in D-day again? Then you can show us your book. Oh, please do!"

And Zan, always fascinated to hear stories about the war, sat down eagerly beside them to listen.

Calm once more, Smoke lay against Zan's legs. The sound and rhythm of familiar voices above him gently soothed him to sleep.

CHAPTER THIRTEEN

Two weeks later, Granpop's condition was noticeably worse. His cough was more persistent, and he was wheezing badly, finding it harder than ever to breathe.

Tebs bent over him, a worried expression on his face. He frowned. "That's it, Granpop! I'm phoning for an ambulance today to take you to hospital."

The old man grabbed feebly at Tebs's hand. "No!" he wheezed. "No, son, I'm not going to the hospital. This is my home, here with you. I'm just so sorry for all the trouble I'm causing."

Beckie knelt down beside him too. "You're no trouble at all, Granpop," she told him gently. "We simply want to see you better. Once you're well again, you can come back home to us."

"If I ever leave here," Granpop croaked, "I shall never come back." And Zan had a feeling that the old man's words might prove to be true.

So Zan bought aspirins, and Beckie bought cough medicine. Tebs and Jake kept the fire going all day long, and at last the old soldier seemed a little more comfortable, although he shivered constantly with the cold.

"What Granpop really needs," Beckie remarked one evening as they sat huddled around the brazier, "is one of those thick, cosy duvets. Are they *very* expensive, Zan?" Nowadays she often turned to Zan for advice or information, and it irritated Tebs enormously.

"Of *course* they're expensive!" Tebs snapped back at her. "They cost more than Zan, or any of us, can afford. A fortune, in fact. We'll have to find more blankets instead. Granpop can have mine in the meantime."

Zan had an idea. "I could get hold of a duvet," he told them. "My own must still be lying on my bed at home doing nothing. I could go and fetch it. It has a rainforest cover. Granpop would love it!"

"Wouldn't you be caught?"

"Not if I go in the afternoon. Dad would be asleep, and Mum out at work. I could meet my sister as she comes home from school." He paused. "Actually, there's something else I need to fetch from Sunfield too. It's Mr. Alassi's fiftieth birthday next week, and he has no one. I've thought of the most perfect present for him!"

"Can I come too?" Five asked hopefully, always ready for a new adventure. "I can show you the best shortcut through the back streets."

Zan decided he might be glad of the moral support. "Yes, all right. We'll go tomorrow."

◆

The waste ground dozed peacefully in the sallow mist of the afternoon. It seemed spacious, almost rural after the noise and clutter of the city. A wide expanse of scrub-covered land, free from buildings and people.

"What a view!" Five exclaimed as they reached the look-out point. He stood for a while, admiring the neat rows of rooftops and city streets. "I bet I can see all the way to Glasgow."

"Fat chance! With *this* smog, you'd be lucky to see as far as Wapping."

At the end of Tin Can Alley, Zan felt his heart beginning to pound. His chest was strangle-tight and his legs were rapidly turning to jelly. It was worse than a visit to the dentist!

"Perhaps you'd better wait here with Smoke," he told Five. "Just in case I run into any trouble."

"Right," said Five. "We'll play sticks, won't we, my old mate?"

Smoke looked unimpressed.

Zan hid a smile. "Poor old Smoke!" he muttered to himself.

◆

The alley seemed narrower than Zan remembered. Soon he was standing apprehensively in front of the house. It looked incredibly neat and tidy. With a new coat of cream paint on the walls at last, and the shutters and window boxes a bright blue, it reminded Zan of a doll's house Kibby had once admired in a museum.

The shed door was unlocked, so Zan went inside. He stood a while, gazing with longing at the wealth of tools hanging on the walls. How useful they would all be, back at the Archway! In the end he settled for a small axe, which was practically his anyway. He would never be reduced to stealing, no matter how bad things got. At least now Tebs could chop up wood for the fire. And Zan might feel safer with it beside him at night.

Kibby's laugh rang out from the road. The sound sent Zan's pulse racing even faster. She was with her friend Lulu, and Lulu couldn't keep a secret if her life depended upon it.

"Oh, *please*, may she go home to tea," he prayed, and was relieved to hear his sister shouting her goodbyes at last.

As she came into the yard, Kibby seemed almost like a stranger – so grown-up in her new navy and grey winter uniform. Her hair had grown too. Now she wore it swept up in a golden pony-tail which reached halfway down her back.

He leapt out of his hiding place, and Kibby shrieked at the sight of a manic-looking scarecrow wielding an axe!

Zan clamped a grimy palm across her mouth. "Shut up, you idiot, it's *me!*"

Kibby prised his hand away and squeaked breathlessly, "Zan! Is it *really* you? Have you come home? How are you? Where's Smoke – is he all right? You've got so *thin!*"

"I'm fine, I've just come to fetch my duvet for my friend Granpop. He's very ill. Smoke's waiting on the waste ground with Five."

"Five *what*?"

"Don't start! There's no time to explain. Can you let me in before Mum comes home? Open my bedroom window! Hurry."

Kibby unlocked the front door and slipped quietly into the house. In Zan's room she struggled with the catch until finally the window was open and Zan was in.

With barely a glance around his room, he began to gather up all the items he needed and pack them hastily into his spare rucksack. He swapped his worn-out trainers for a pair of old walking boots. They still fitted him, thank goodness, and they would be much stouter and warmer for the winter.

"Any chance of a sandwich, Kibs?" he asked at last. "I've really missed your specials." Kibby scurried out to the kitchen.

Zan looked impatiently at his computer. "What a useless piece of equipment!" he said aloud with some disgust. "Can't eat you, can't wear you . . . ." Had he been able to carry it, he might have been tempted to sell it, or exchange it for something a little more functional.

Kibby returned after a short while, bearing a large plate piled high with thickly cut wedges of bread. "Wow!" said Zan with a grin. "Double-doorsteps at least!"

"Cheese, pickle, and tomato ketchup!" she informed

him, with a mock grimace. "Your favourite. Yeuch!"

"You're a superstar!"

"And here's a carton of milk, too. I expect you'll be thirsty."

"Brilliant!"

Zan perched on the bed and began to wolf down the food. Kibby sat beside him, taking in her brother's strange new look. His chubby face was so much thinner, almost gaunt. It made him look older, and a lot more mature. But the less said about his long hair and grimy fingernails, the better!

After a short silence, she spoke. "Zan, *won't* you stay? It's horrible here without you. Dad's not nearly so grumpy nowadays, but they argue about you. And sometimes I can hear Mum crying when she thinks I'm asleep. We all miss you so much."

"What about Smoke?"

"He can go to Rowan Park. There's a wonderful wood-land enclosure just waiting for him over there. With other wolves for company. Oh, Zan, he'd *love* it! Matthew says he's growing up, and he needs to be a wolf again."

"It's a trick," Zan said.

"No, honestly, it's not!" cried Kibby. "Matthew's really nice – you'll like him when you know him properly." She paused. "Jenna misses you dreadfully too," she tried next. "She's jolly thin. Toby helps me feed her sometimes."

"That's another reason I'm here. I've found her a home, Kib. Somewhere she'll be loved, with so much food, she'll never be hungry again!"

"Oh," said Kibby flatly. She had run out of ideas. In a moment of desperation she wondered whether to wake up their father and tell. But she knew her brother would never forgive her if she did.

Zan wiped the ketchup off his chin and licked his fingers. "Got to go," he said, tucking the last sandwich into his pocket for Five. "Mum'll be back soon." He tugged the duvet off his bed and pushed it out of the window. Then he climbed carefully after it.

Kibby leant out and thrust three ten-pound notes under his nose. "Here. These were in the kitchen jar. I'm sure Mum'd want you to have them."

"Thanks, kid!" Zan said. "I promise I'll keep in touch this time." And then he was off up the alley, holding the bulky duvet up off the ground as he ran.

"I'm not kid," she called after him. "I'm *Kibby!*"

In a matter of seconds, Kibby could hear her mother's bus arriving at the top of the road. She quickly shut the bedroom window and went back to the kitchen. Sitting down at the table, she began to pull homework out of her school bag. When her mother came in, she was lost in concentration.

Yet again, she had to allow Zan plenty of time to make his escape.

◆

While Five tucked into his sandwich, Zan scouted around the outskirts of the waste ground, whistling for the collie.

Then, cupping his hands around his mouth, he called, "Jenna! Jenna! Here, girl!" as loudly as he could.

Smoke heard the distant barking first, and in no time a black and white whirlwind was hurling itself at Zan, almost knocking him right off his feet.

In a frenzy of acrobatic leaps, wagging tail, and frantic licking, the little collie greeted first Zan, then Smoke, then Zan again, as if they had been gone for a hundred years or more.

Five looked on with amusement. "She's sweet!" he said, by now truly a dog lover. "A much better-sized dog! Can we keep her? Here, girl."

"No, she's for Mr. Alassi's birthday! He'll love her."

"If you can ever persuade Tiza to part with her. She'll go soppy, I know she will."

Zan slipped the length of rope he had brought around Jenna's neck and handed the other end to Five. "You can take her. Let's go!" he said, grinning with satisfaction. "Mission accomplished!"

But then his smile froze. Barring their path stood a gigantic black ogre of a creature, yellow teeth bared and hackles raised.

"Cripes!" exclaimed Five, making sure that Zan was between him and the evil apparition. "What the blazes is *that?*"

"That," said Zan succinctly, "is Thor!"

The huge mongrel growled a threat, and at once Smoke ran forward in response.

"Quick," Zan told Five urgently, "take Jenna and the

duvet and wait on the road. I think they really mean to fight! And I'm not sure if I can stop them."

"Be careful, mate, or they'll tear you apart!"

The angry wolf closed in on Thor. Zan was astounded to see how much Smoke must have grown in the past few months. Now that Smoke was no longer a pup, Thor saw him as a serious threat to his leadership. Battle was inevitable!

Smoke was not play-acting either. The two creatures leapt towards each other like snarling demons.

"No, Smoke! NO!" Zan cried out, wrenching off his rucksack and hurling it at them. But Smoke ignored him. Locked together, the two warring animals rolled over and over, snarling in rage and pain.

Zan felt sick and shaky as he looked on. "Stop it! Please stop!" he screamed helplessly.

Suddenly, a volley of barking from two other members of the alley pack distracted Thor's attention for just a second.

Seizing his chance, Zan plunged in, grasped Smoke's red collar firmly, and hauled him away with every ounce of strength he possessed.

Then the wolf turned on *him*. Savagely, Smoke grabbed Zan's forearm tightly between his massive jaws, threatening to bite right through his jacket to the bone.

"Smoke!" Zan choked out a last desperate appeal to the enraged creature.

But as he looked into the wolf's fiery eyes, Smoke was

not there. Instead there was a wild creature he did not know, maddened by the challenge, blinded now to everything else around him, driven only by his natural instinct to fight for superiority. It was as though anything they had ever been to one another had never existed at all.

Then, just as suddenly, the old Smoke was back. He dropped Zan's arm, casting it aside almost apologetically, and returned his full attention to Thor.

But the black mongrel backed off, still growling ominously. Like a departing thunderstorm, he raced away across the waste ground.

"Quick!" shrieked a frantic Five. "Let's get out of here before Godzilla changes his mind!" And with Jenna at his heels, he ploughed off up the road at a mad gallop, with half the duvet trailing along on the ground behind him.

As the street lights came on above them, Zan gingerly led Smoke away. The wolf was still growling quietly too, but at least he was under control again.

The boy, however, had been shaken to the core. For a few devastating moments, the sweet gentle creature who had been his soul-mate for what seemed like a lifetime had been replaced by a savage stranger he didn't recognise at all.

Soon the wolf was trotting affably along beside him, feathery tail tip wagging as he moved. But Zan knew that the unshakeable trust and understanding they had always shared could never be quite the same again.

That afternoon, something priceless had been lost forever. And suddenly their future together was looking a little uncertain.

CHAPTER FOURTEEN

Granpop was delighted with the duvet. The old man had not been so cosy since the summer months, and the warmth seemed to ease his pain. His apparent comfort was a great relief to everyone.

Each day, one of the group stayed behind to keep the fire going and provide hot cups of tea boiled up in an old enamel kettle which Zan had found on a market stall. He often bought useful things on his way home from work, and even Jake had ceased his jibing. Necessities and the odd luxury had made life a little easier for them all.

One chilly afternoon, it was Zan's turn to stay and keep Granpop company. Everyone else had gone out, including Five and Tiza, who had taken Ziggy and a much-pampered Jenna for a run by the river. Smoke always stayed with Zan, no matter how tempting the outing.

The boy was seated on a rickety wooden chair close to Granpop's mattress. He was reading aloud from *Wings of the War.* As the old man listened, he dozed peacefully on and off.

Clip clop, clip clop. For a moment, the noise sounded remarkably like a two-legged horse trotting down the tunnel towards them.

"Must be a stranger," Zan thought. "No one from around here wears high heels like that!"

The stranger came into view. She was a pretty young woman, dressed in a white mackintosh. Tied loosely around her neck was a red and gold scarf which half hid her thick chestnut hair. She looked dramatically out of place in the murky depths of the Archway.

"Good afternoon, may I help you?" Zan asked.

"Zan, and Smoke, I presume!" she announced cheerfully.

The boy's mouth gaped open in amazement.

"I'm Tansy, Tansy Briar. I'm a journalist with the *Sunfield Satellite.* I've been following your story for months, ever since the day you first found Smoke."

A fleeting look of something like relief seemed to pass over the boy's grubby face, but then his expression changed to one of deep suspicion. "How did you find me?"

"Kibby mentioned an old man called Granpop. So I made some enquiries and eventually found my way here. My goodness, your street people certainly protect their own, don't they?"

"You've been talking to my sister? She *swore* she'd never tell!"

"Please don't blame her, Zan – she misses you dread-

fully. And your parents have been frantic with worry!"

"You'd better sit down," he invited, pulling an orange box closer to the fire.

Tansy positioned herself as comfortably as she could, but she could already feel the splinters snagging her new tights.

"Come home, Zan," she urged gently. "If not for your sake, then for Smoke's. Matthew says he'll be fully grown soon. He's not a pup any more, and he'll *never* be a dog. He'll become more and more unhappy living like this."

At the mention of his name, Smoke whined, nudging Zan's shoulder with his nose. Wanting attention. Needing reassurance.

Zan, remembering the terrible fight with Thor, reflected that Tansy was probably right. Nowadays, Smoke did seem more restless, more fretful, than when he was younger. But the thought of losing him raked like an eagle's talons across the boy's chest.

"Kibby told me about the huge woodland enclosure at Rowan Park," he volunteered gruffly. "So it's not a trap, then? He won't be put in a cage, to be stared at?"

"No, of course not!" Tansy protested. "The sanctuary's a terrific place to live. Smoke has lived with humans too long, so he could never survive in the wild. But he can be happy at Rowan Park."

The young journalist could see the first flicker of interest in the boy's eyes, so she let the matter rest. There was no point in pushing him too hard. He'd been through enough.

"Tell me all about the others who live here with you," she prompted, and then listened intently as he did so. For of course it was quite a tale.

"And what about Granpop?" Tansy enquired finally.

Zan gestured towards the ground nearby, where the old man lay sleeping under the rainforest duvet. His face was haggard, his breathing uneven.

"Oh, the poor soul!" Tansy exclaimed softly. "He really should be in hospital, Zan, receiving proper care. This is no place to be ill. To be honest, it's no place to be *well* either!"

"We've all tried. He won't go," Zan informed her. "He wants to stay here, with his friends. He said he'd rather die here."

His companion looked so concerned that the boy added hastily, "Honestly, he does seem a bit better since I fetched my duvet. He sleeps more soundly, and his cough has definitely improved. It's not nearly so hoarse."

Tansy rose slowly to her feet, with only a fleeting glance at the ladders which were racing each other down her tights. She sighed. "They were very old ones anyway."

"I was just going to make some tea," Zan offered, by way of compensation. "Won't you stay for a cup? The milk was fresh last Tuesday."

"No, thanks – I really must be going," the young woman replied. "Now, Zan, I shan't put any more pressure on you right now. But I'll come back in exactly one week's time and see if you've made your decision. And until then, you have my solemn promise that I won't breathe a word of this to anyone."

She looked him steadily in the eye and he believed her.

She stroked Smoke's soft head several times, then turned and walked briskly away.

Granpop stirred slightly and shuffled over onto his side. Zan was not aware of it, but the old man had been awake, and he had heard every word Tansy had spoken.

◆

Mr. Alassi's fiftieth birthday dawned bright and clear. The city streets were packed with eager Christmas shoppers. Often Zan found himself pushing through the throngs, wistfully aware of exciting-looking parcels and seas of happy faces, glowing with festive anticipation.

The department store windows were ablaze with intricate displays and colourful decorations. The main streets were festooned with Christmas lights. Zan, Beckie, Tiza, and Five always stopped to admire the show on their way home to the Archway. Anything free in this world was well worth enjoying.

That morning, the four had stopped by a skip permanently parked in a side road. Anyone on the street knew it was a good idea to check if anything usable had been discarded. People threw away a lot of useful things.

"Maybe Mr. Alassi would like this!" Beckie pulled out an ancient porcelain chamber pot, ornately decorated with bright pink roses.

Tiza gave a squeal of laughter. "I can't possibly give him a po for his birthday, Beck!"

"Why not? They cost a fortune down in Darby's Antiques. And there's only a tiny chip in the rim."

Zan was busy delving among the rubbish too. "There's a reasonable-looking plant under that box," he remarked. "A sort of ivy, I think. Why don't you plant it in the pot?"

"It would give a whole new meaning to 'potted plant'!" teased Five, and Beckie threw a mildewed cushion at him. Their good-natured laughter filled the deserted street.

After lunch, Zan and Tiza brushed Jenna's black and white coat until it shone, then fastened a blue ribbon around her neck. Their excitement was contagious, and before long Ziggy, Smoke, and the little collie were all cavorting about like mad creatures.

By the time everyone was ready to go, the whole party looked surprisingly presentable. Beckie had even persuaded Zan and Five to let her tidy up their hair for the occasion. It was to be the older girl's turn to stay with Granpop. She had said, very generously, that she didn't mind missing the outing, but everyone knew that secretly she did.

They set off at five-thirty with Smoke and the dogs. Tiza was clutching the rather battered potted plant as if her life depended on it. And, gentlemen to the last, not one of the boys offered to carry it for her.

Tebs was whistling a current hit song, and Zan's spirits were high in anticipation.

Mr. Alassi was in for quite a surprise!

◆

The kindly Italian had been feeling depressed all day. As nobody had remembered his birthday, there seemed little point in having one. He had closed up the restaurant after lunch, for he didn't feel like working that evening. Instead, he sat at the kitchen table, head in hands, dreaming of the good old days with his family back in Siena.

A sharp rap on the back door sent Mr. Alassi leaping to his feet. Suddenly he remembered he had invited Zan to bring Tiza and Five round to meet him. However, he had not really expected them to come.

Hastily he opened the door, and stood astounded as a crescent of friendly faces smiled up at him. Surely it was too early for carol singers?

"SURPRISE!" they chorused. And it was.

Zan stepped forward. "Happy birthday, Mr. Alassi! I've brought some extra friends with me. I do hope you don't mind? You said we could come."

Tiza solemnly presented the astonished Italian with her ivy, perched precariously in its rose-painted pot. "This is for you," she said, relieved to have delivered it in one piece. "It's an antique."

"It's a gezunder!" said Five, with relish.

They waited for a reaction, and when it came, it was spectacular! Mr. Alassi set down the plant and flung his arms around Tiza's neck. He kissed her heartily, three times on each cheek, then hugged her tightly, almost suffocating her in the process.

"Ah, *grazie*, my little one, *grazie*," he cried. "Is beautiful – the most beautiful thing I ever see!" He kissed them emotionally, each in turn, including Tebs and Jake, whose red faces were a glorious picture of embarrassment! Mr. Alassi's smile was dazzling. It was as though the sun had come out.

"Oh, Zan, you are a good boy! You remember old Carlo after all!"

Zan grinned. "Of *course* I did. And I've got something special for you too." He gently urged the little collie forward. "This is Jenna. She's one of my very best friends, and she needs a good home. I'd like you to have her."

Mr. Alassi struggled to speak. He clasped and unclasped his hands several times. Then, to everyone's astonishment, tears began to roll down his cheeks. He spoke in a voice trembling with passion, his English growing worse by the minute. "For me? Oh, Zan! Oh, *bellissimo!* A million thank-yous! I am come over with thankfulness!"

Bending down, he clasped the collie's pretty face gently in both hands and gave her a huge smacker of a kiss, right on the muzzle. "*Cara mia!*" he sobbed, and Jenna wagged her tail politely, her good ear cocked at a lopsided angle.

Zan was rather moved by Mr. Alassi's display of emotion, but Five had been seized by an uncontrollable attack of the giggles, and Tiza was struggling valiantly not to succumb too. Zan glared at them. It seemed so impolite!

Tebs turned away quickly, pretending to cough, while

Jake awkwardly scuffed his feet on the cobblestones.

"You hungry? I cook for you, *si?*" wept Mr. Alassi ecstatically. He pulled out a voluminous white handkerchief and blew his nose loudly, like a ship's foghorn. "Come in – I make you my special Alassi sauce!"

"A Lassie sauce?" Tebs hissed to Jake in horror. "Does he really think we're expecting to eat poor Jenna now?"

Zan elbowed him hard in the ribs. This was, after all, the invitation he'd secretly been hoping for! "Thank you, Mr. Alassi. We'd love to stay," he enthused. "Wouldn't we?"

And of course the answer was a resounding "Yes please!" from everyone.

The friendly chef proved himself to be extraordinarily generous. What a feast they had that night! Mr. Alassi cooked mountains of fresh pasta, awash with rivers of his famous tomato sauce.

Smoke, Ziggy, and Jenna were guests of honour, with their meals served up on the very best china plates.

When everyone was full enough to burst, their genial host asked hopefully, "You like *gelato*, yes? Some ice cream now, eh?" Then, before anyone could answer, he vanished. When he reappeared, he was carrying glass dishes heaped high with a mouthwatering selection of Neapolitan ices.

Five beamed across the table at Zan. He rolled his eyes skywards, for once beyond words. It was the dreamiest, creamiest ice cream he had ever tasted. Absolute heaven!

When the tables were finally cleared and the washing-

up done, Mr. Alassi brought out a battered old record player and a stack of 1950s rock 'n' roll records. They were mostly his favourite, Elvis Presley. As only he and Jake knew how to jive, they jived together. Mr. Alassi's face flushed an even deeper shade of crimson with the exertion, and his arms flailed about in the air. The others clapped along, laughing and cheering, until their ribs ached.

Tiza proved to be a natural dancer. Soon she and Jake were spinning around the restaurant at breakneck speed, with Smoke racing in circles behind them.

"*Bravo, molto bravo!*" cheered Mr. Alassi with delight from the sidelines. He hadn't enjoyed himself so much in years.

"The first wolf ever to jive to Elvis, I'll bet!" Zan mused to himself. "If only Matthew Harding could see him now!"

Tebs played his harmonica, performing wonderful versions of "Hound Dog" and "Jailhouse Rock." Then they all sang, and then they danced some more, until everyone was completely exhausted.

At last, sadly, it was time to leave. Mr. Alassi waved an enthusiastic goodbye to his guests from the back doorstep. Their laughter and happy voices spilled out across the cobblestones and into the cold night air beyond.

"*Ciao*, Mr. Alassi, and *grazie!*"

"*Grazie* to you, my friends! What a wonderful birthday you give me. I never forget it!"

As he reached the corner, Zan hardly dared glance behind him. He had been worried Jenna might try to follow. However, the little collie knew which side her bread, or rather her pasta, was buttered. She had found a wonderful new home, and she wasn't budging an inch! Her future looked positively *bellissimo!*

Tail wagging like a clockwork toy, she stood silhouetted in the doorway beside the portly frame of Mr. Alassi. He gave one final windmill wave. "Goodnight, Zan my boy. You too, Smokey old fella. See you soon, eh?"

Zan waved back. Then, with Smoke bounding at his heels, he ran to catch up with the others.

CHAPTER FIFTEEN

 Beckie was waiting anxiously in the entrance to the Archway. Her face looked white and strained under the street lights.

"Thank goodness you're back at last," she told Tebs. "Come quickly. Granpop's much, much worse."

"We've done all we can for him. Now we really must fetch a doctor," he decided. Shaking away the exuberant memories of their earlier festivities, he tried to think clearly. "Damn it! The nearest working phone is down at Bridge End."

"If I cut through the grounds of the toy factory, I could reach the hospital in minutes," Jake offered calmly. "Maybe I could persuade someone to come straight back with me."

"That's an excellent idea," Tebs agreed, and without another word, Jake vaulted nimbly over some nearby railings and disappeared into the darkness.

Zan and Five coaxed the dying embers back to life and soon had a roaring fire going again. Beckie and Tebs knelt over the ailing Granpop.

"Shall I fetch some aspirins and a nice hot drink?" Tiza asked.

Beckie shook her head. "No, we'll just try and keep him warm 'til the doctor arrives," she said quietly.

"No doctor!" gasped Granpop stubbornly.

Tebs patted his hand. "This time – yes," he said. "No arguments!"

It was obvious to Zan that the old man was really struggling for breath. He was wheezing almost like an asthmatic.

"D'you think he has pneumonia?" Five asked nervously. He was lingering awkwardly in the background, scared to come too close to Granpop's mattress for fear of what he might see there.

"I don't know, Shrimp," answered Tebs. "Let's wait and see."

They waited for what seemed like hours. The only sounds were Granpop's laboured breathing and the occasional train passing overhead. Someone was singing "Land of Hope and Glory" drunkenly in the distance.

"Zan," Tebs said suddenly, "I think Granpop wants to speak to you."

At once Zan scrambled over to where the old man lay. He perched on the edge of the tattered mattress and took Granpop's cold bony hand in his. "Yes, Granpop? It's me, Zan. I'm here."

Granpop was trying to speak again, frustratedly forcing out the words between his desperate efforts to draw breath.

"I can't hear you, Granpop." Zan leant even closer, until his ear was almost touching the old man's lips.

And then he *did* hear. Just three simple words, so insistent despite such frailty, and all the more precious for the momentous struggle it took to utter them. "Go... home... son!"

Then, quite suddenly, Granpop seemed much better. Zan couldn't hear him wheezing at all. His breathing was quiet. His hand relaxed its urgent clasp, and his wrinkled old face looked almost youthful. Tranquil, and at peace.

Zan glanced up hopefully at Tebs. "Is he sleeping peacefully at last?"

Slowly, Tebs leant back and sighed. "It's no good, mate. He's gone."

Zan was stunned. "Gone?" he repeated. Then, as the full realization hit him, he leapt to his feet and shouted, "NO!" His cry echoed around the Archway until it faded into the inky gloom of the night. "NO... no... no...."

Beckie began to cry, and Five, realising at last what had happened, wailed hysterically.

"Do shut up," Tebs told him curtly. "That dreadful racket won't bring him back."

He looked over at Zan and their eyes met briefly. The boy felt a hundred years old.

"Better get tidied up around here," Tebs said quietly. "I

expect Jake'll be back with the doctor soon."

Smoke whined fretfully, pawing at Zan's trouser leg. He sensed that something was terribly wrong.

◆

Later that night, they all sat round the fire, numbed by the shock of Granpop's death, bereft at the loss of such a treasured friend and guardian.

Nobody said much. It was hard to know what to say. But Five sat very close to Tebs, and Beckie had her arms tightly round Tiza and Ziggy. One by one they crept away to sleep, and to be alone, until only Zan and the faithful Smoke were left, huddled together for warmth and comfort.

The boy was staring into the dying red embers of the fire, lost in his grief, feeling suddenly so weary, and so totally alone. In two days' time Tansy would be returning. Again and again he heard the old man's quavering voice, appealing to him, determined, insistent. There was a great deal of serious thinking to be done.

But deep in his heart, he knew that he had already made his decision.

Zan moved closer to the wolf. Putting both arms round Smoke's thick, furry neck, he looked deep into his amber eyes. There, at least, the days always seemed to be of endless summer.

"There's something I have to do, old fellow," he told him quietly. "It doesn't feel like the right thing, but now I think it must be. The problem is, it means we can't be together any more."

Smoke was staring back intently, ears pricked, intelligent eyes puzzled, trying to understand every word. Or maybe he already did.

"Now that you're nearly full-grown," Zan went on, "it's not fair to keep you on a rope and expect you to behave like a dog, out here on the streets. You're a timber wolf. Your spirit should be wild and free – running with your own kind, not with me.

"Smoke, you're the best friend I've ever had, and I want you to know that I love you more than anything else in the entire world. But soon I'm going to take you to Rowan Park, where...."

His voice broke, and he couldn't say any more. One solitary tear escaped and worked its way through the grime on his right cheek. Concerned, Smoke whimpered and licked it away. His touch felt warm and reassuring.

"Oh, Smoke, you'll never know how hard this is."

The wolf's gentle gesture was too much for Zan. He buried his face deep into Smoke's soft coat and, for the first time in years, he began to sob like a child.

◆

Clip clop, clip clop. Zan heard Tansy before she came into sight, as her brisk footsteps brought her marching rapidly along the tunnel towards them. This time, the journalist was wearing jeans with her high heels. She clutched

two bulky carrier bags, one in each arm.

"Hello." The young woman smiled sympathetically at the little group in front of her. "I was so sorry to hear about poor Granpop. I know you all did everything you possibly could for him."

Tebs acknowledged her condolences with a grateful nod and a gruff "Thanks."

"I've brought along a few supplies to keep you going," Tansy went on. "Dried stuff, mostly – porridge oats, some rice, biscuits, and packet soups."

"How kind of you." Beckie gratefully commandeered the carrier bags before the boys could get their hands on them. Five's passion for chocolate biscuits was world famous. He could eat his way through two packets of digestives without a twinge of conscience or indigestion.

Tansy took a piece of paper out of her handbag. "Now then," she began in a business-like manner, "I've been chatting to a friend of mine, Sue Simpson, who runs an excellent halfway hostel not far from here. She says she can find beds for Beckie, Tiza, and Five by next week. You might like to stay there for a while. She's awfully nice, and I know she can help all three of you back onto your feet again."

"I'm not leaving Ziggy," protested Tiza.

"You don't have to," Tansy assured her. "Sue loves dogs – she has three of her own. They're all completely barmy! Here's the address."

Beckie tucked the piece of paper carefully away in her

pocket. "Thanks, Tansy," she said. "We'll go and see her tomorrow."

The journalist turned her attention to Tebs. "You *are* Sebastian Carrington-Smyth, aren't you?" she asked quietly.

Tebs hesitated. "Yes," he admitted finally, "I am."

"Your father, Lord Granbrook, has been searching the ends of the earth for you," Tansy told him. "*Please* ring him, Tebs. I don't know what happened between you. But at least let him know you're all right. You too. Jake – why don't *you* phone home as well? It doesn't take a minute."

Tebs and Jake exchanged knowing glances. Jake said nothing.

"Maybe," said Tebs. And that was the best Tansy could hope for.

Then she looked at Zan. There was no need to ask if he had come to a decision. She could see that he was ready to go with her. "All set, then?" she asked, a little too brightly.

Zan felt a sudden pang of fear clutching at his stomach. This was the moment he had been both dreading and, in a strange way, longing for.

He hugged Tiza and Beckie. "I'll be in touch," he promised, and Tiza began to cry. So many sad goodbyes in such a short time.

The boy shook Jake's hand, and then turned to Tebs. "Thank you for everything," he said sincerely.

"You're not such a bad lad!" Tebs grinned, aiming a playful punch at Zan's chest.

Zan glowed. Now he felt like one of them!

Lastly, he came to Five. Taking off his watch, he solemnly handed it over. "This is for you, Five. You'll never be late again!"

"For *me?* Thanks, mate!"

And, on the spur of the moment, Zan also slipped off his walking boots and slid them across the ground towards his best friend.

Five beamed and slipped them on with a flourish. To his delight, they almost fitted him. "Aren't I the well-dressed city gent now?" He minced back and forth in front of the others, and they all laughed at him.

"They're *miles* too big, Shrimp!"

"You look like a clown!"

"Come on then, Zan," Tansy urged at last. "Matthew will be waiting for us." Turning, she headed off into the tunnel. Zan and Smoke followed, padding silently along a few feet behind her. Zan didn't dare look back.

The icy north wind bit right through to the bone as they reached the market. Tansy fished about in her handbag and produced some money.

"For heaven's sake, go into that shop and buy yourself a new pair of shoes!" she told Zan. "I can't possibly take you home in those revolting lime-green socks!"

Zan hesitated. "Oh, but I couldn't – you've done so much already."

"Just *do* it, please," Tansy ordered firmly. "All I'd like from you Zan, is for you to tell your story. And I need your help to try and get the others off the streets before Christmas."

Within moments the boy was back, proudly sporting the cheapest and most garishly coloured training shoes he could find. He handed Tansy the change. Can't afford! *Now* he'd tell his school mates all about 'can't afford'! Purple and orange? Great shades! And a brand name he'd never *heard* of before, but he didn't care that the shoes weren't the right designer make. The springy rubber soles transformed the pavement underfoot into thick, deep-pile carpet. As he followed the young journalist to the kerb, it was like walking on air.

Tansy whistled up a taxi in a most unladylike fashion. As it pulled alongside, the driver tugged down his window and warned ungraciously, "No dogs!"

In a final un-Zan-like act of defiance, the boy yelled at him, "He isn't a dog. He's a WOLF!" Five would have been proud of him!

There was little left for the astonished driver to say. Quickly opening the door and trying hard to hide her amusement, Tansy climbed in, followed by Smoke and Zan.

"Rowan Park Wild Animal Sanctuary, please," she ordered primly. The driver hastily shut the glass partition and steered the taxi away from the kerb. He wasn't going to argue with a wolf!

Zan opened his window and looked back. He could just make out Tebs, Tiza, and Five standing among the people milling around the entrance to the Archway. Already it looked like another world.

Frantically, he waved, and they waved back. As the taxi pulled quickly out into the traffic, the figures grew smaller and smaller, until at last they were swallowed up by the crowd.

CHAPTER SIXTEEN

 The taxi driver drew up outside the imposing wrought iron gates of Rowan Park. It was a vast estate. While Tansy paid the traumatised driver, the gatekeeper telephoned through to the main office to notify Matthew Harding of their arrival.

Zan curled his index finger through Smoke's collar. The gesture was more for his own security than anything else. Well, this was it! For one mad moment, he wondered whether to turn around, with the wolf, and run.

Smoke looked up at him confidently and wagged his tail. He could detect exciting new animal scents on the wind. The air smelt fresh and clean. The wide open spaces of the sanctuary were a far cry from the grimy depths of the inner city they had left behind them. Above the wooded hillside, the sky was a deep, endless blue, and the tepid winter sun poured across the fields towards them like a river of liquid gold.

A camouflage-painted jeep pulled up beside the gates.

The door opened and Matthew Harding climbed out. He kissed Tansy and shook Zan warmly by the hand. Then he bent down to make an enormous fuss of Smoke. The man petted the big wolf with the ease of someone well used to handling exotic animals.

"Magnificent!" Matthew rose to his lofty height and gave his verdict at last. "And I can hardly believe how tame he is! He could do with putting on a bit of weight," the biologist observed, "but he's in remarkable shape for a wolf who's been raised on the streets!" His friendly manner made Zan feel more comfortable.

Matthew Harding outlined his plans as he drove towards the main complex. "We'll call in to the surgery first. Jill, our vet, can give Smoke the once-over. She'll need to run some tests just to make sure he has a clean bill of health. Of course, he'll have to stay in quarantine for a short while, and then you can come and let him out into the main woodland enclosure. Maybe on the day, Tansy could bring along a photographer from the *Satellite* too. I'm sure it'll be quite an event!"

Zan took in everything that Matthew was saying, but somehow he felt detached from it all. He realised that it was because the whole matter had finally been taken out of his hands.

From the very first second he had cradled Smoke as a tiny, helpless pup, the wolf had been dependent on *him* – his responsibility alone. But now there was so little left for him to do. He had to allow Matthew to take over. But it was hard.

The jeep passed a small group of zebra standing beside the fence, munching their way through a large bale of hay. Freed from the nightmare confines of their circus pen, they were living the life of Riley in the spacious, grassy park.

"Stupid creatures," Zan thought uncharitably. "What sort of a life have *you* ever lived? Have *you* ridden flat out on an empty milk float? Eaten cold pizza for breakfast under the railway? Danced to Elvis Presley in an Italian restaurant?" Hot tears threatened to fill his eyes, and he had to blink very hard to clear them away.

He glanced over at Smoke. The wolf was clearly enjoying the drive. His ears were cocked, his eyes glittering, fixed on the road ahead. He was panting slightly with excitement.

"Oh, Smoke, how am I going to live without you?" Zan thought. "Life will be so different for both of us."

◆

The quarantine pen was quite spacious, with a small cosy shed in one corner. A large, bare section of treetrunk lay across the central section. Matthew opened the gate and ushered Zan and Smoke inside.

The boy knelt down and slowly unbuckled Smoke's red leather collar. Putting it carefully into his pocket, he gave the wolf a brief hug. His coat smelt of antiseptic from the surgery. Smoke's normal, comforting smell had already diminished.

"Let's leave him to settle in," the biologist suggested,

"and Caroline can bring him some food. Has he eaten today?"

"A prawn sandwich, and some sherbet lemons."

Matthew Harding managed not to laugh. "I thought we could drive out to the wolf sanctuary, if you'd like to inspect it?"

"Yes, please," answered Zan, rather subdued now.

◆

Icy daggers of wind stabbed through Zan's duffle coat as he scanned the woodland enclosure. It was much larger than he had expected – several acres, no doubt. The other boundaries weren't even in sight. A wide expanse of winter grass rolled sweet and green across the pasture, rising to a small hillock on the right-hand side. From the top there must have been a spectacular view east, towards the city.

"Look! You *are* honoured!" Matthew exclaimed suddenly. He handed Zan his binoculars. "Over there, by the thicket – *canis lupus* – the fabulous timber wolf!" He pointed towards a dense piece of woodland on his left. "Can you see them, Zan?"

Zan adjusted the field glasses. They came to rest upon a pair of sleek creatures standing cautiously at the edge of the trees. The animals were smaller and more lightly built than Smoke. One was creamy, almost pale apricot in colour, but with bandit markings like Smoke's. The other was a much darker greyish-brown.

"The lighter one's Elsa – she's something of a rarity. We

named her after Joy Adamson's lioness. The darker one's Sheba," Matthew continued.

Zan stared hard at the wolves who would become Smoke's new family.

"Quite a welcoming committee, aren't they?" joked Matthew, and, despite his mixed feelings, Zan had to laugh.

◆

When they arrived back at the quarantine area, Caroline the keeper was delivering a large stainless steel bowl filled with raw meat.

Smoke wagged his tail in welcome as she entered the pen. Then he began to gulp down the food.

Matthew smiled. "A good sign. His Majesty seems to be making himself at home already!"

As Smoke ate, Zan stood and watched for a while, with his nose pressed hard into the wire netting until it hurt. Finally the boy turned and started to make his way slowly back towards Matthew and Tansy. But after a few steps, he spun round again.

The wolf looked up abruptly from his food. For a few intense seconds, their eyes met, and their minds seemed to be locked together in some form of telepathic communication. It was almost as if Smoke was finally releasing him. Then the wolf put his head down and resumed his meal.

Zan tried to walk on. But each step became more and more difficult to take. It was as though his entire body had been filled with concrete. He bit his tongue, not wanting to let Matthew and Tansy see him cry.

Catching sight of the boy's stricken face, Matthew patted him gently on the back. A sympathetic grin glinted through his beard. "It really *is* for the best, Zan," he said. "He must learn to be a wolf again. Smoke is a wild animal, not a pet. He wasn't born free. This is the best thing you can do for him."

Zan wanted to stamp his feet and scream out loud, "I *know* it's for the best; I can see that it is! But how does that help *me*, when I feel as though my heart has been clawed from my chest and the wings have been wrenched off my soul?"

A deep mental and physical ache was spreading through him, worsening with every inch he moved away. And, had it not been for Matthew's steadying hand guiding him along the pathway, he might well have wandered off in a daze, back to a twilight existence on the city streets. Something so precious, something he had been waiting for all his life, had been given to him, only to be taken away again, after what seemed like a fleeting instant in time.

What was the point of going on?

"You can come and see him," the biologist said encouragingly. "I'll have a special staff pass made up for you. Though, to be honest, it will be better if he's gradually weaned off his dependence on human company." Seeing Zan's stricken look, Matthew added, "Of course, I'll need

your help at first. We could make a start next week, if you'd like."

Tansy slipped a protective arm around the boy's shoulders and gave him a gentle squeeze as the three of them ascended the steps which led up to the main reception area.

"Now then, young Alexander," she said, "there are some people here who, I think, might be quite pleased to see you!"

Zan looked up, and his heart leapt as he saw his mother, his father, and Kibby standing there.

June Makepeace gave a little cry of joy as soon as she set eyes on her son. But she seemed frozen to the spot.

Sam Makepeace hesitated at her side, unable to make the first move either.

It was Kibby who broke the ice, throwing herself into her brother's arms and nearly knocking him right off his feet. She hugged him so tightly he could scarcely breathe.

"How strong you've grown!" Zan mused, half-heartedly pretending to pull away. He didn't realise that it was partly because, over the months, *he* had become so much weaker.

At last the delighted Kibby released him and drew back a little. Then, wrinkling her freckled nose, she declared, "STRONG? *You* can talk! Your clothes smell so disgusting, they could walk home on their own!"

With the suddenness of a balloon bursting, the tension was gone, and everyone began to laugh with relief.

EPILOGUE

 New Year's Eve was crisp and frosty. Uncle Kevin and Aunt Josie had returned home with Grandma after the long Christmas break, and peace was at last restored to the household. Only the decorations remained as a final reminder of the past weeks' festivities.

For Zan, it had been a bittersweet time. The oppressive heating, the noise, all the gifts, and the sheer volume of unwanted food had overwhelmed him. Frequently, he felt as though, instead of returning home, he had been transported to a different planet. His thoughts often drifted back to the Archway. And at the forefront of his mind, for nearly every waking second, was the nagging ache of parting from Smoke.

His bedroom looked alarmingly clean and tidy. Antiseptic. A little like a hospital, Zan thought. But it provided him with a welcome refuge from the well-meaning attentions of his family and the smothering amount of love being lavished upon him.

He retreated there whenever he had the chance, to take advantage of some much-needed solitude. And to lie on his new African safari duvet and read.

That New Year's Eve afternoon, he was engrossed in the wonderful natural history book which Matthew Harding had given him for Christmas, when there was an eager tapping on the bedroom door.

"Zanny, can you come *now?*" called Kibby. "We've a surprise out here for you!" Her voice was filled with mystery.

"Go away, please, Kib. I'm reading."

"But *Zan*, it's *urgent!*" Kibby insisted.

Intrigued, Zan followed his sister out to the sitting room, where his parents stood side by side with secretive smiles on their faces.

"Over there, over *there!*" Kibby was dancing up and down with excitement. "It's a surprise present."

Underneath the Christmas tree stood a large cardboard box with several holes cut in it. It was tied loosely with lengths of silver tinsel. The parcel seemed to be moving very slightly. It also seemed to be making an awful lot of noise for a cardboard box. Zan glanced warily at his mother. He felt confused. Trust was not something which came easily to him nowadays.

"Go on, Zan," she encouraged him. "Hurry up and open it. It won't bite! Well, at least I *hope* it won't!"

Zan had barely opened the lid of the box when he was

bowled right over backwards by something small and soft which yelped and yapped and covered his face with a shower of warm, wet licks. Such a familiar greeting, and what memories it brought flooding back!

It was a PUPPY! A cocker spaniel puppy, with the most gloriously shiny red coat he had ever seen.

It jumped and bounced, accidentally hitting him on the nose. It ran round and round in circles, tripped, and rolled over. Then it launched itself at Zan again in a frenzied puppy greeting, as the Christmas tree wobbled precariously. The boy stared at these antics, speechless with amazement. And then he began to laugh with delight – really laugh, for the first time since he had come home. He laughed until there were tears streaming down his cheeks.

"She's all yours, son," said Sam Makepeace, his deep voice soft with emotion.

Zan could barely speak, but he managed to blurt out, "Oh, *thank* you, everyone! Thank you *so much!* She's brilliant! I think I'll call her Ruby!

"Ruby, Ruby!" squealed Kibby, enchanted.

And Mrs. Makepeace could only look on, her eyes bright with relief.

◆

It was a few minutes to midnight when Zan, with Ruby tucked snugly inside his jacket, climbed quietly out of his bedroom window. The ground was slippery with frost as he jogged carefully along Tin Can Alley towards the waste ground. His breath formed vapour clouds in the bitter night air as he ran.

From the highest point on the waste ground, there was a clear view right across the city. As midnight chimed from a nearby church, the boy was aware of an unseen tide of celebration. It swept over the rooftops in rippling waves of cheering and singing, of people embracing, of hopes and resolutions for a brave and exciting new year.

In several distant places, fireworks soared up into the inky skies, leaving in their wake spangled trails of gold and silver. It seemed to Zan that an interplanetary war was raging in the heavens above him.

Then, after a few minutes, everything stopped as suddenly as it had begun, and a new, precious stillness settled over the city.

"Happy New Year, Ruby," Zan whispered, as he cuddled his puppy closer to him. "And Happy New Year, Smoke!"

He took a deep breath of cold, night air, raised his eyes towards the moon, and howled. Then he held his breath, straining every nerve, every fibre, to catch any hint of a response. He howled again, filling the atmosphere with an eerie and unearthly sound, so wolf-like that the waste ground upon which he stood could have become the Canadian wilderness.

Was that the faintest cry he could make out, in the far, far distance? Reaching across all those miles of concrete roads and houses towards him? Linking him with his soulmate; mind to mind, and spirit to spirit? Joining them together again, one last time, in a final, sweet dance of freedom? Or maybe it was only his imagination.

A dog began to bark in a house nearby, and a light came on in an upstairs window. Ruby was growing restless, and she began to whine and wriggle. Zan reassured her, then turned and slowly retraced his footsteps home along the frosted alley.

◆

A few moments after Zan had climbed into bed, there was a tap on the door and his mother came in.

"Zan? Happy New Year! I saw your light on, so I knew you were still awake. I've brought you some hot milk and chocolate cake. Kibby's fast asleep already, but I've saved her some for tomorrow."

The puppy began to trampoline joyously up and down on the bed, her tiny, silly tail wagging her entire body in an ecstatic welcome.

"Ruby, you little monkey!" Mrs. Makepeace said with a smile. "Now, Zan – we had a deal, didn't we? The puppy sleeps in the kitchen."

Zan reluctantly relinquished Ruby, and Mrs. Makepeace tucked the squirming puppy firmly underneath her right arm.

"'Night 'night, dear," she murmured. She pulled the door shut, then opened it again, poking her head back through the doorway. "And Zan," she added, in a voice so low it was almost a whisper, "I'm so glad you're home."

" 'Night, Mum."

Left alone in his room again, he stared at Smoke's red leather collar lying on the bedside table. Restlessly, he switched on the radio. There was an old Kalynda Kingham song playing, and the sweet words and gentle music filled him with emotion.

It's hard to say goodbye, though you've been gone a
*   while now,*
I live that final moment a dozen times a day.
But the hours we spent together seem to be another
*   lifetime.*
It'll take another lifetime
Just to ease my tears, and chase the fears away.

Zan stretched out an arm and reached down into the void underneath his bed. Suddenly, he could feel the strong, warm rasp of Smoke's tongue on the palm of his hand. So familiar, and so reassuring, just as though he were really there. And now Zan knew that he always would be.

ABOUT THE AUTHOR

While confined to bed with chronic fatigue syndrome, Melanie Jane Banner began to write short stories, animal articles, and poetry. Smoke is her first published novel, and it reflects her love for the natural world and the environment. Ms. Banner gained so much pleasure from her childhood reading that she wanted to "give back some of that pleasure to today's children, in the hope that they too might continue to believe in the magic of a world rather less materialistic than the one in which we now live." Melanie Jane Banner lives in Surrey, England, with her three cats, Jet, Dusty and Clover.

ABOUT THE ILLUSTRATOR

Kveta freelances for magazines, advertising agencies, book publishers, and other clients. Her studio, Kveta Illustration & Design, is located in Markham, just north of Toronto. She works in a wide range of styles and techniques including watercolour, pencil, pen and ink, airbrushing, computer illustration, and graphic design. As a wolf lover, Kveta was very excited to be involved with the production of *Smoke*. Kveta also teaches art, privately and through local organizations.